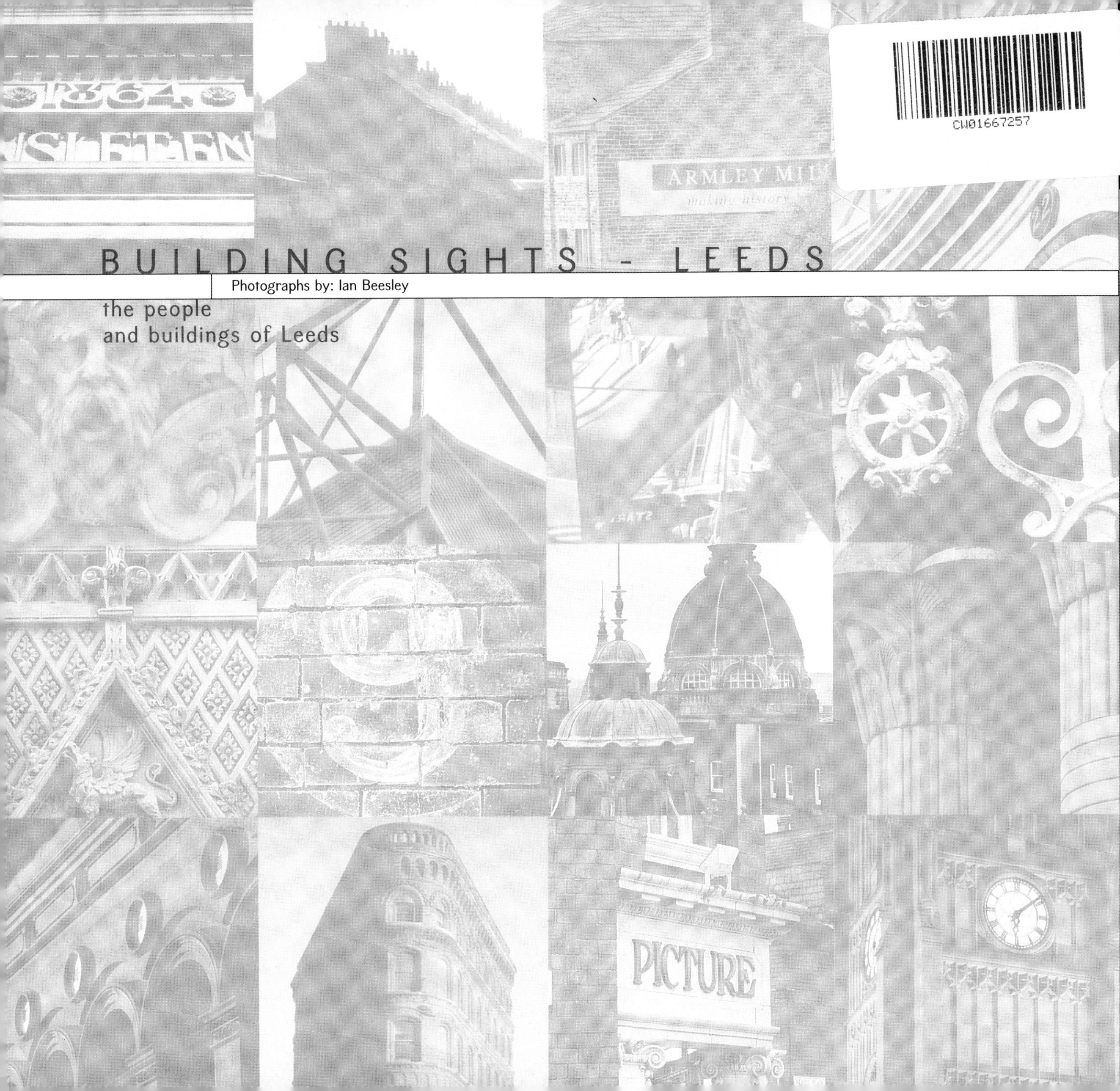

BUILDING SIGHTS - LEEDS

Photographs by: Ian Beesley

the people
and buildings of Leeds

BUILDING SIGHTS - PHOTOGRAPHS BY IAN BEESLEY

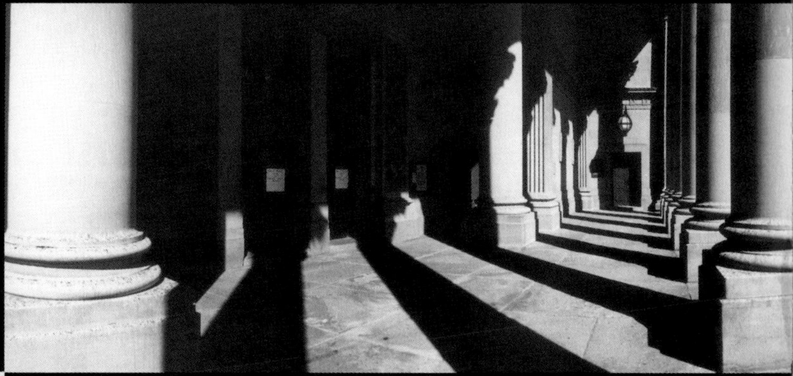

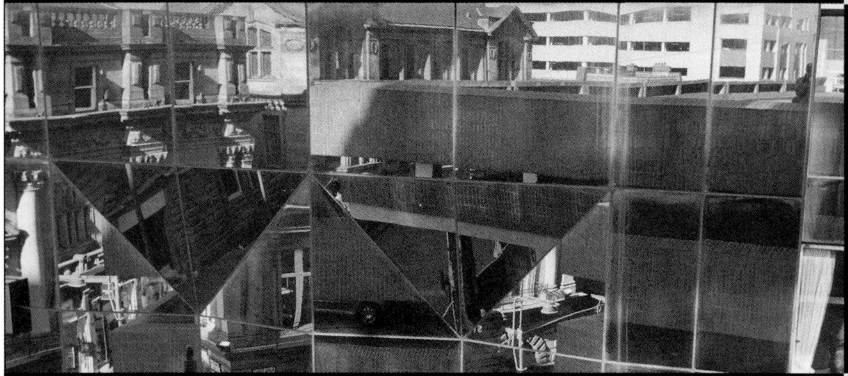

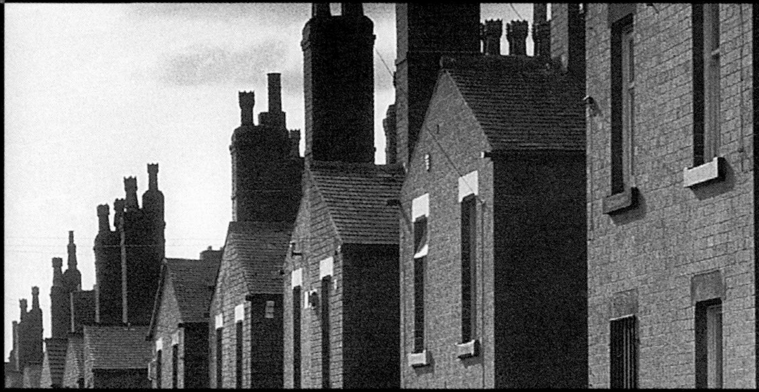

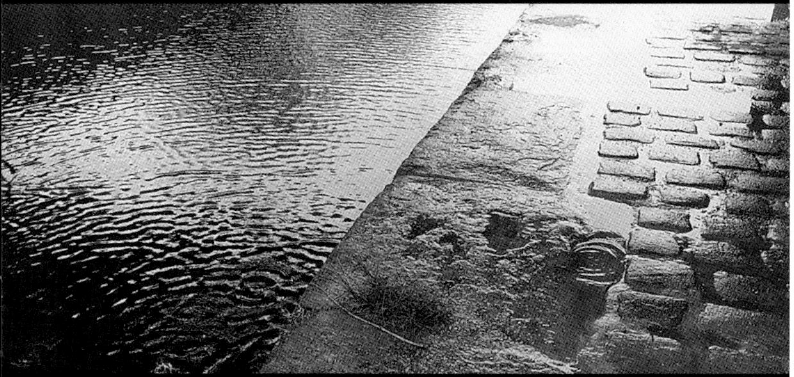

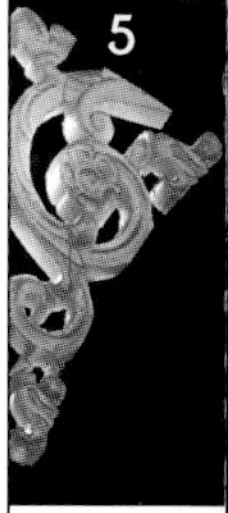

BUILDING SIGHTS

Photographs by: Ian Beesley

Which buildings in Leeds have played an important part in your lives? This was the question that the curators of the Leeds Industrial Museum put to the people of Yorkshire in the year 2000. We wanted to know just what real-life stories were tied up in our city's rich stock of buildings. And you were quick to respond.

During the following months letters came in thick and fast giving us an amazing picture of life in Leeds over the past eighty years. From the dramas of dressing for the dance hall to romance in a public park and from the sheltering columns of the Town Hall to the allure of allotments, it was all here. Your nominations proved just how important our buildings are as guardians of memory and experience ; the dullest bit of brick and mortar comes to life when it is embedded in someone's personal history.

Choosing a short list was hard work for all of us. The range of options included buildings as diverse as elegant Temple Newsam or the well built 7th Airedale Scout Hut. Ugly or beautiful, it was your stories that counted and thanks to the labours of photographer Ian Beesley, words and images have come together in this present exhibition and publication. We hope that it jogs a few memories or inspires you to create a few new ones of your own!

Above all our work shows that buildings, though beautiful, cannot be considered in isolation. Work places and schools, markets and clubs, act as a backdrop to our lives and interests. Ornate stucco and elaborate shop fronts are nothing on their own. As one of our contributors said "Its the people inside that count". And hopefully that's what Building Sights is all about.

Daru Rooke

Senior Curator of Social and Industrial History, Leeds Museums and Galleries

March 2001.

DANCE HALLS

Built: 1930's	The Empire, formally The Astoria, formally The Harehills Palais.	Location: Harehills Corner.

"I love dancing, I'd dance every night of the week if I could, I've been all over dancing, Armley Baths, The Astoria, The Town Hall.

I learnt to dance at Mark Altman's Dance Hall, opposite Leeds General Infirmary. It would be in the 1920's. Everyone went there to learn, he was famous in Leeds for teaching dancing. He had a great big hall, lasses would stand on one side and the boys on the other side "You've come here to learn to dance, and that's what you'll do or you can go" he used to say, he could get anyone to dance.

I was in tailoring so I used to make all my own dresses, my dad used to complain that I went out dancing too much "Stop dancing or I'll burn all your dresses" he said, I put them in a big pile in the middle of the room and said "Go on then" I wasn't bothered because I could soon make some more".

Betty Barker

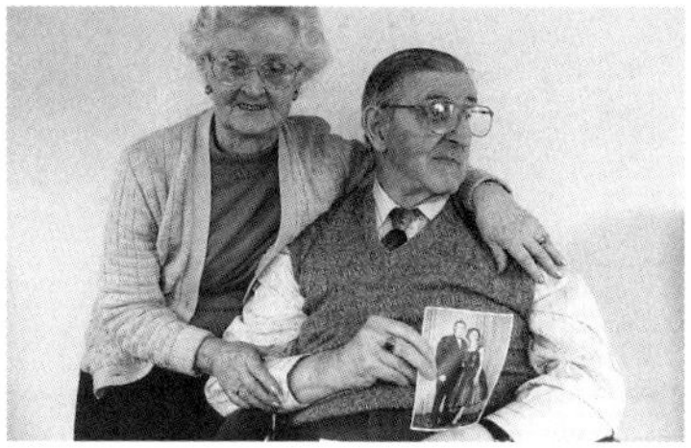

" Mark Altmans, it was a scruffy hole, there were no good dancers there. I went to the 101 Club, Westminster buildings. It had a beautiful dance floor and good dancers. Admission was 9 pence during the week and 1/3d on a Saturday"

Bill Johnson

"Mark Altmans was where you went to get a man, all the dances were 'excuse me's'. Mark Altman would say to you "If you can't get a man here you can't get a man anywhere". That's where I met my husband, my mother came down the steps and said to me "There's only one man up there who can dance", well that was Bill he was a beautiful dancer, I don't know what he was doing there that night ?"

Muriel Johnson.

"I was slumming it".

Bill Johnson

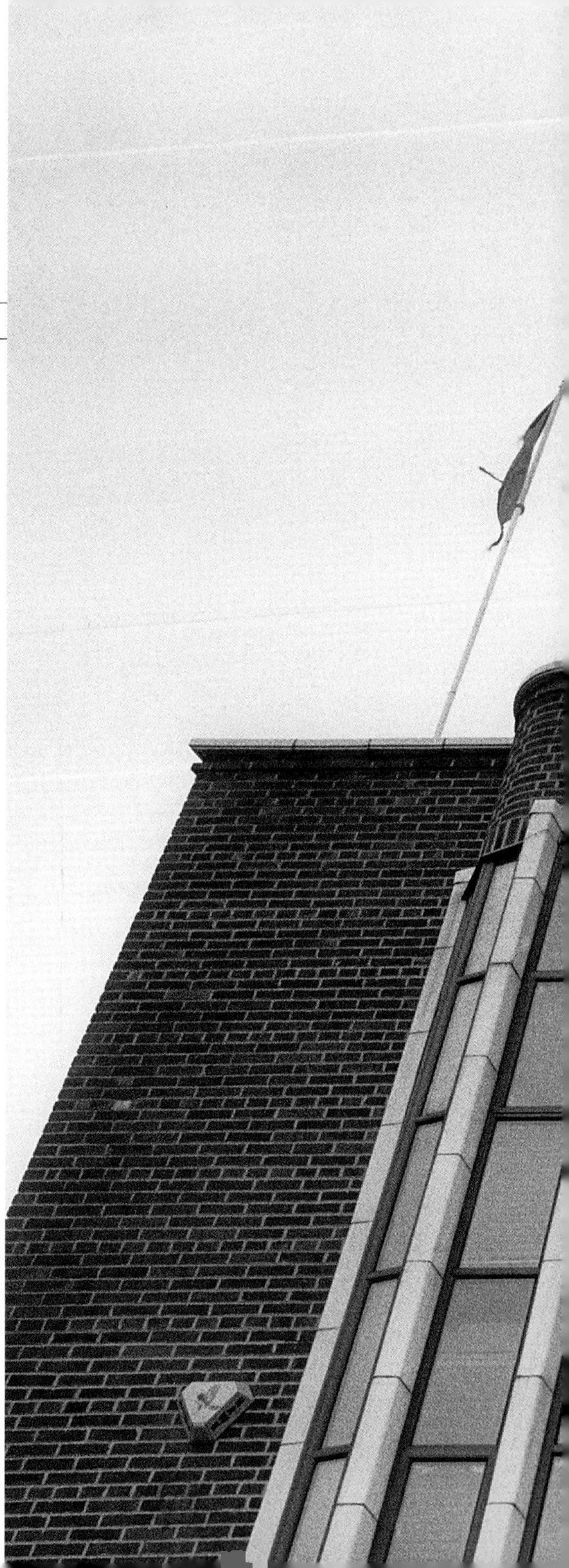

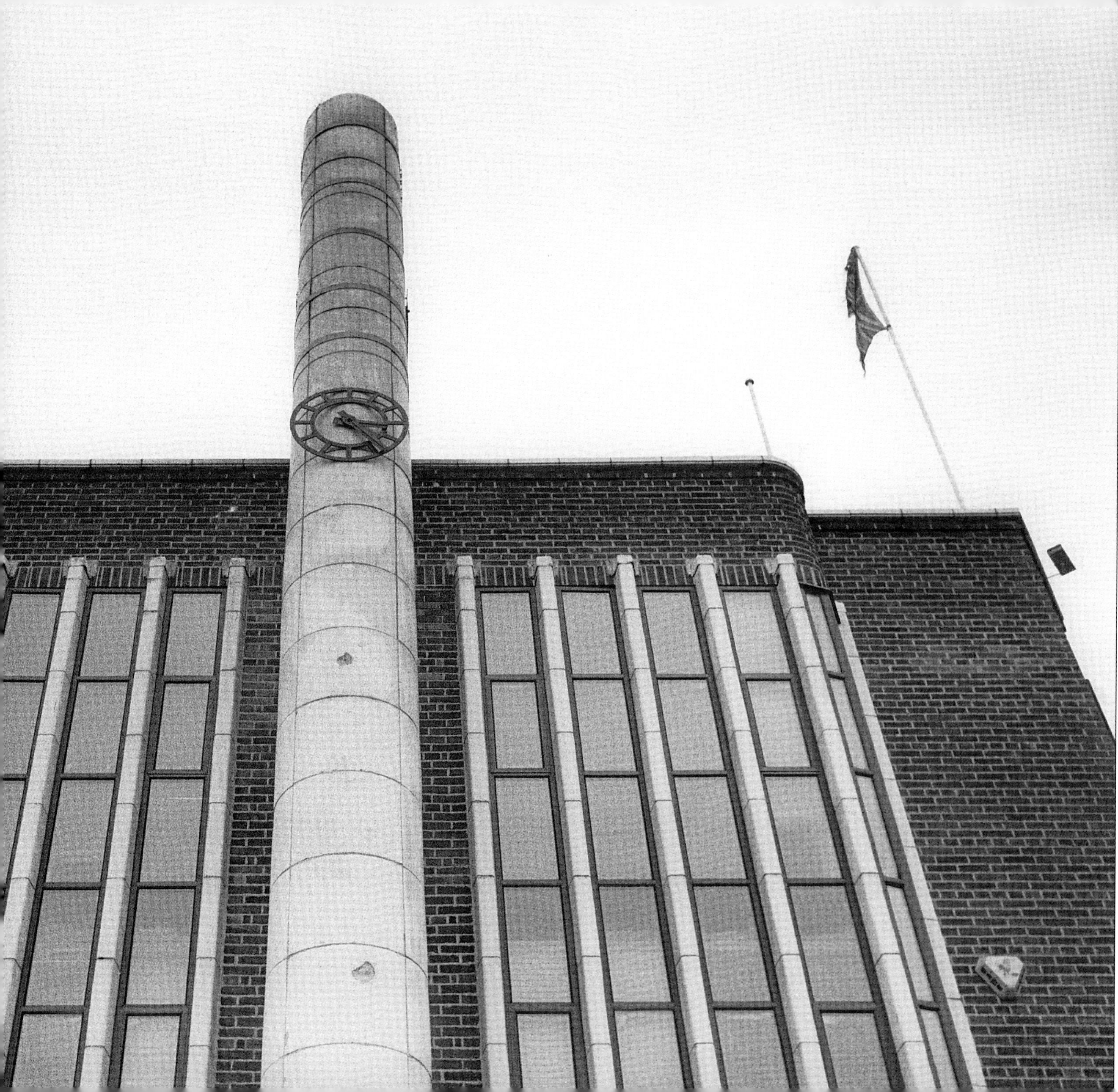

THE CORN EXCHANGE

Built: 1861-63 Cuthbert Brodrick.	Location: Call Lane.

"I pass the Corn Exchange on my way to work by train everyday and - whatever the weather, from brilliant sunshine to deep snow its marvellous outline, texture and details never fail to lift the spirit".

David Bowcock

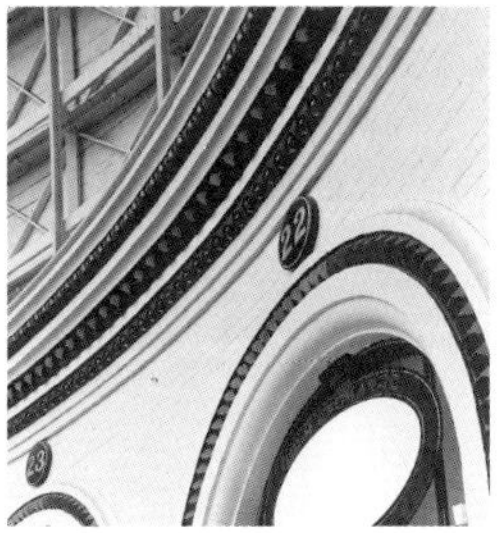

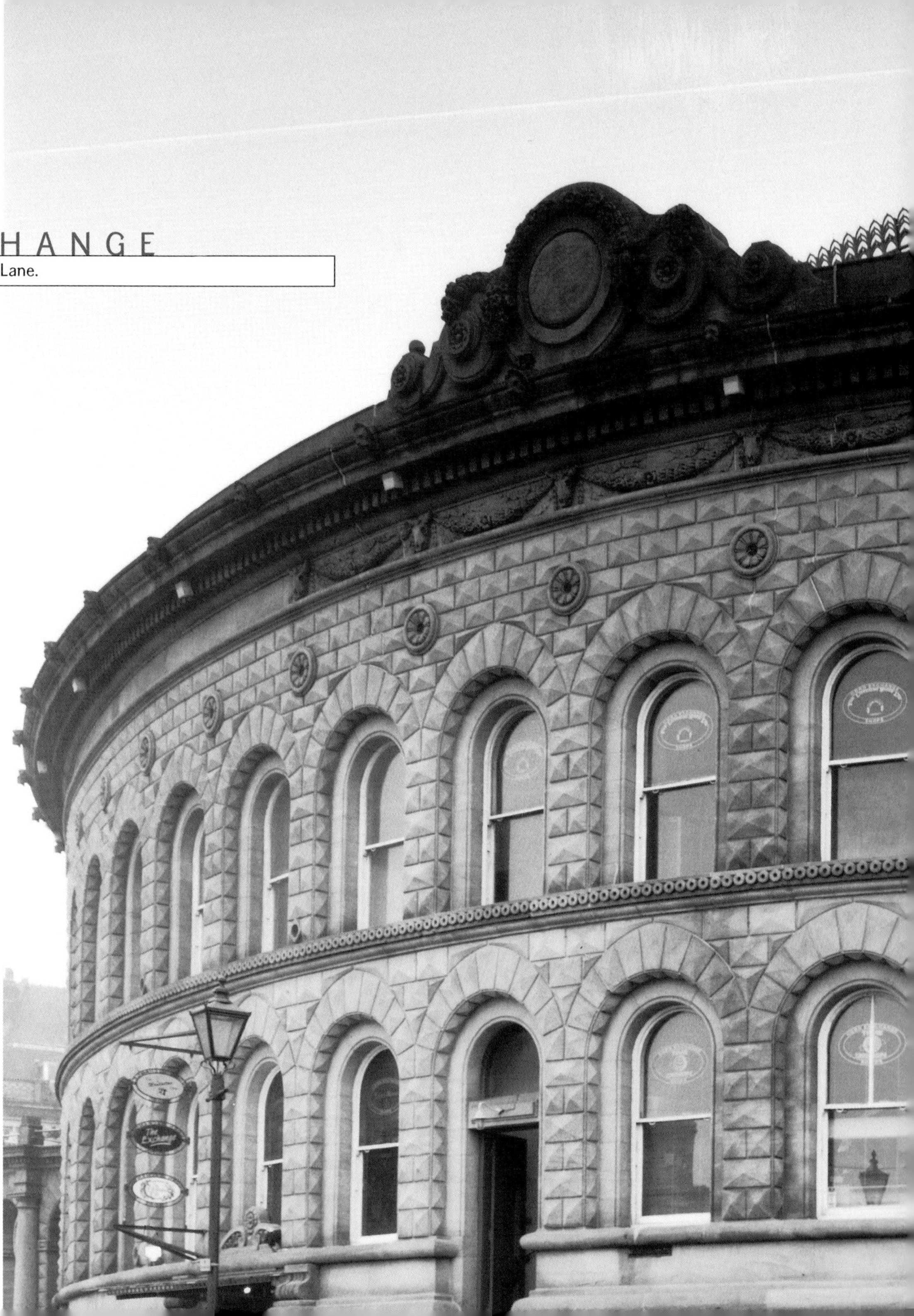

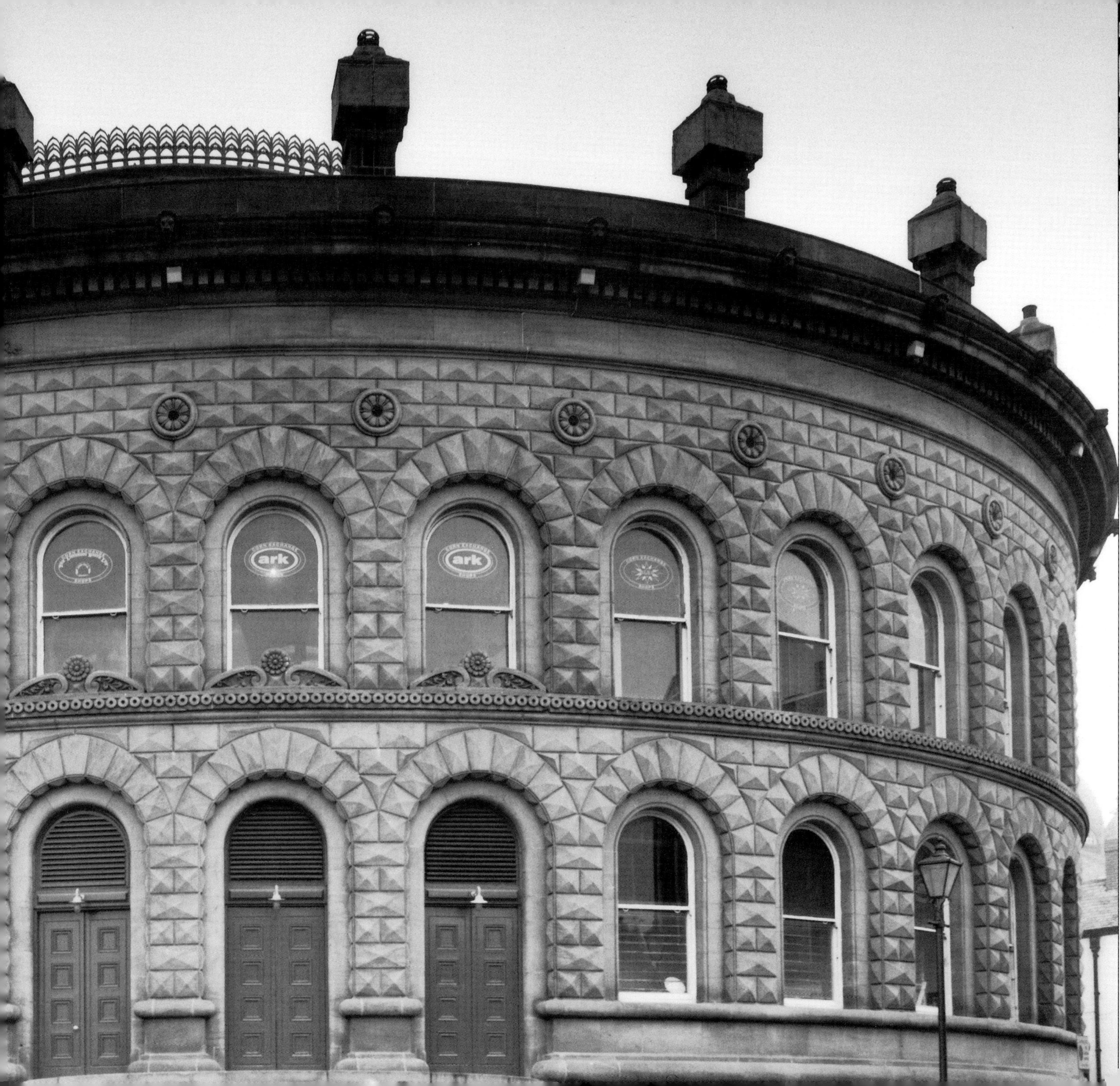
ark
ark

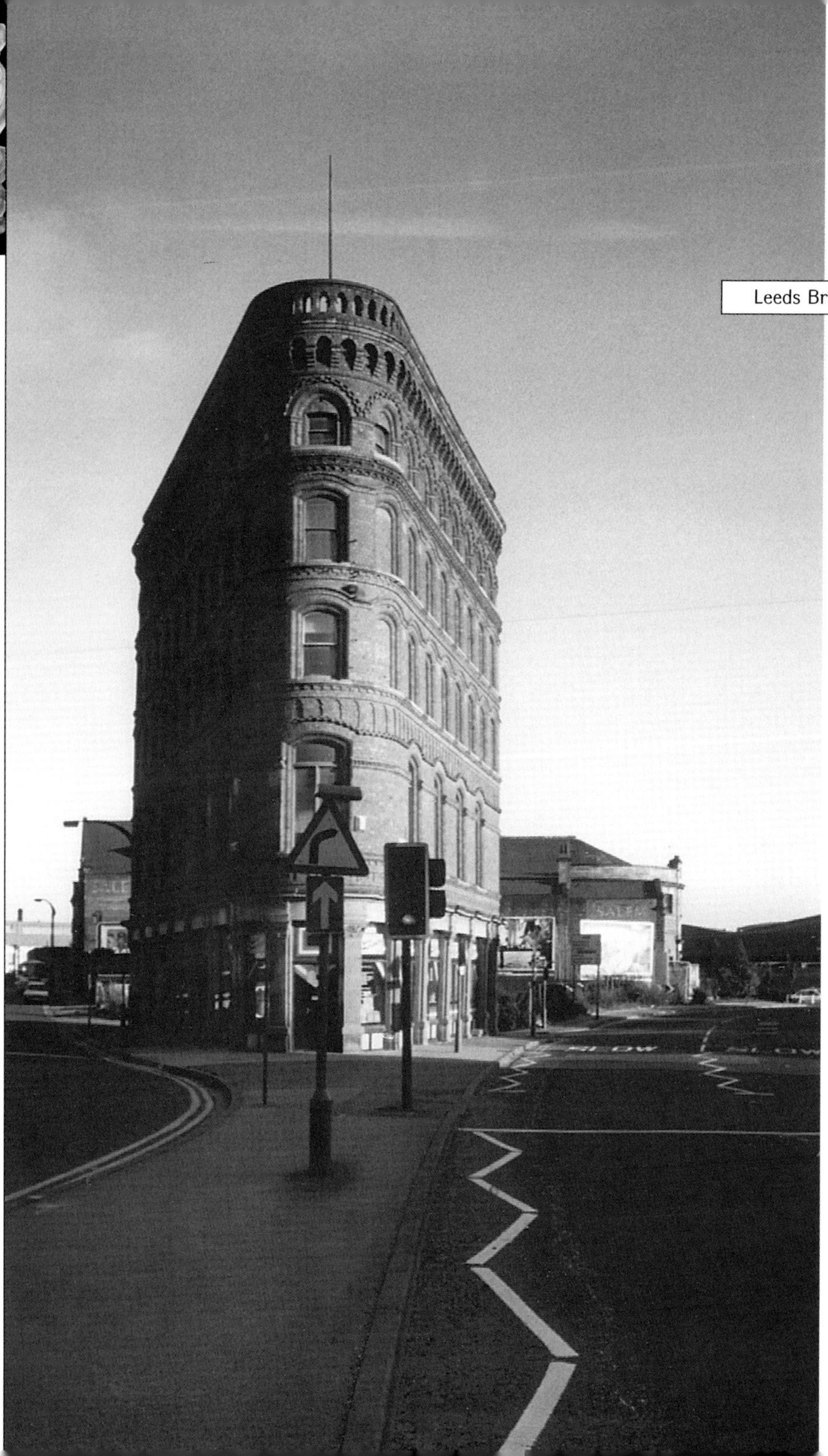

FLAT IRON BUILDING

Leeds Bridge House	Location: Hunslet Road

"I call it the Flat Iron Building because it reminds me of that famous one in New York, the one you see on all the posters, I don't know which one was built first, but I would like to think it was this one and the Americans copied it".

Jennifer Bailey

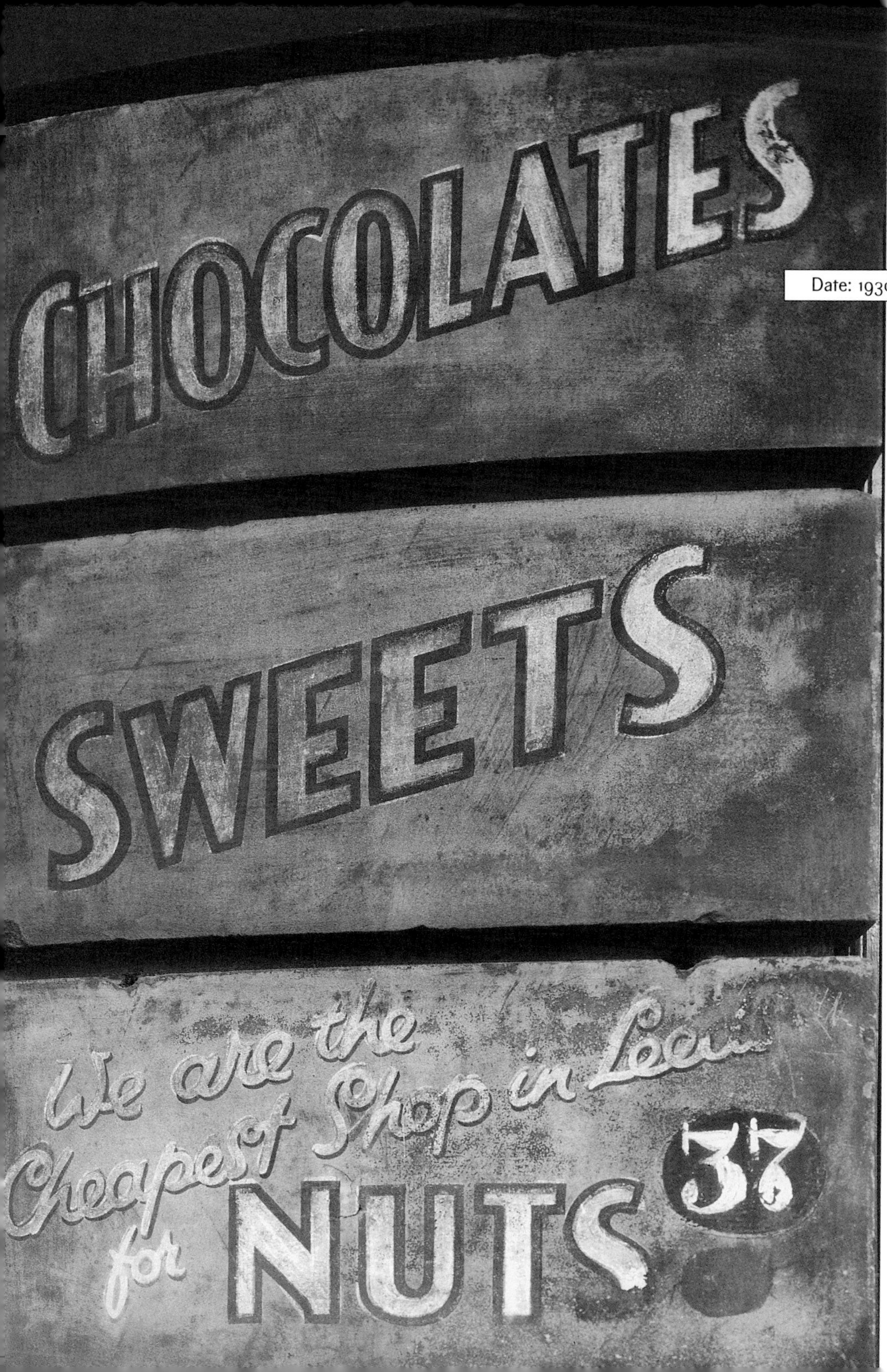

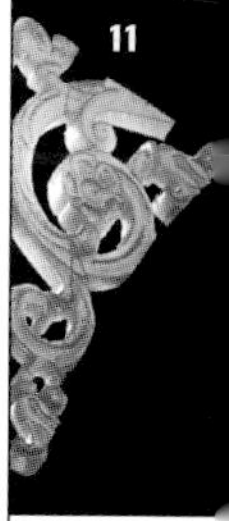

SWEET SHOP DOOR

Date: 1930's	Location: Corner of Cookridge St. and George St.

"You had better be quick, cos we are going to sandblast it all off "

Construction worker

KIRKGATE MARKET

Rebuilt: 1903-04 Leeming and Leeming.	Location: Kirkgate.

" I've been here best part of 9 years, it's a lovely building, but the market is knackered, no customers. They don't come like they used to do, they don't have to come into town no more. It's all that out of town shopping that's done it, they can get everything they need. I might as well jack it in and go work for Asda or B&Q, I'd probably make more money".

Ryans Fruit Stall Manager

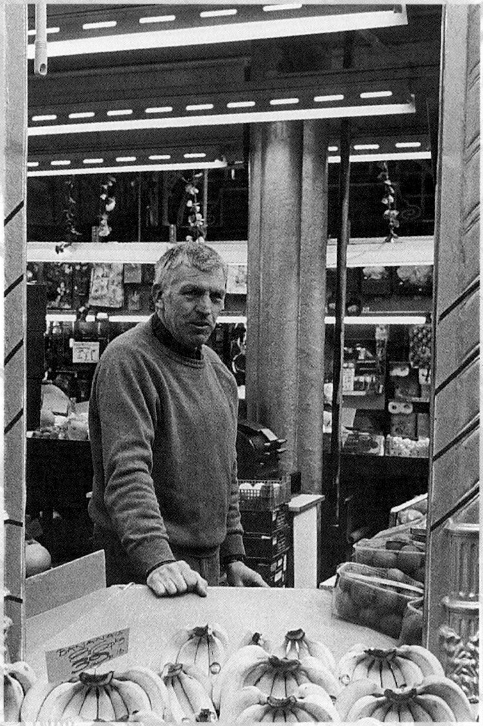

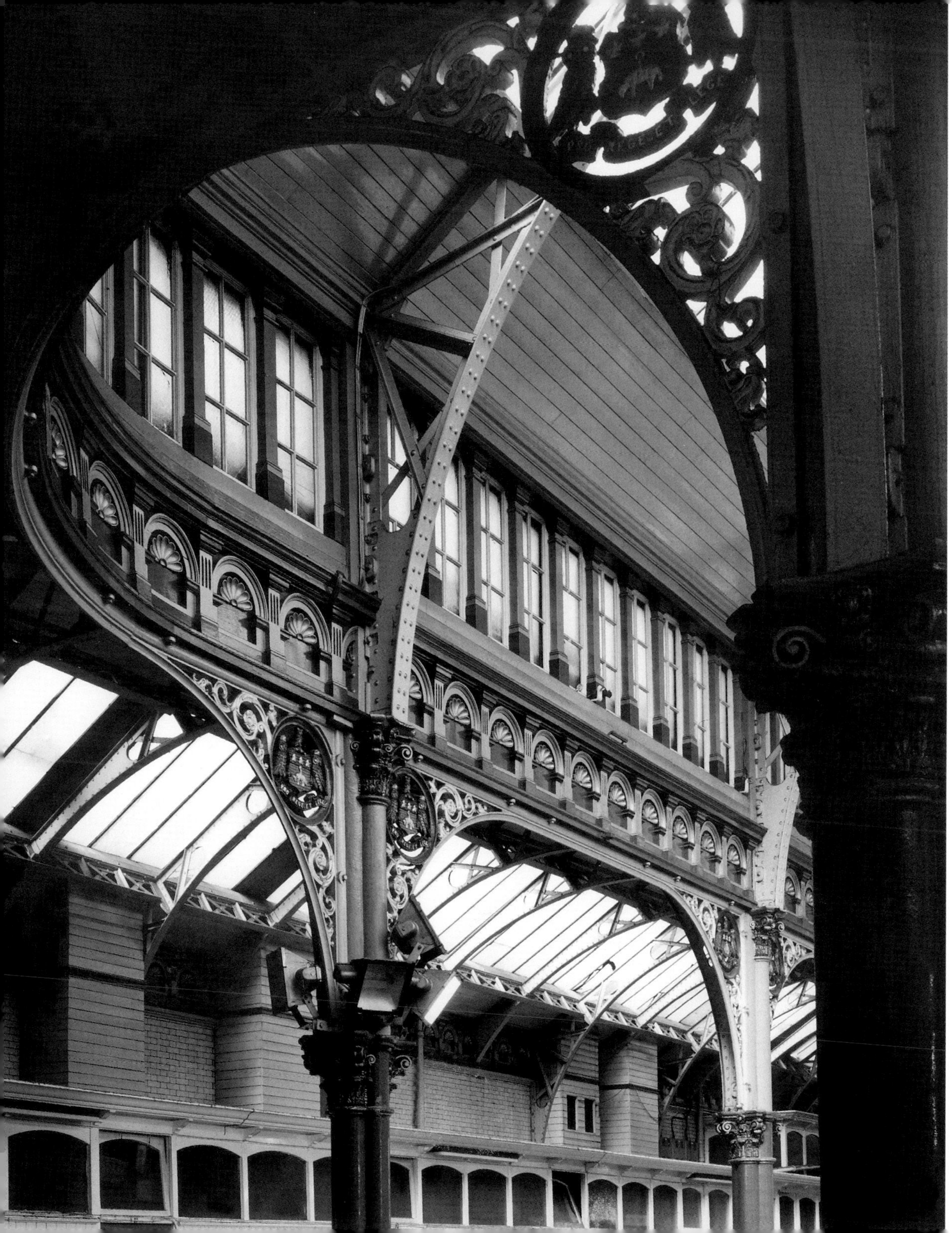

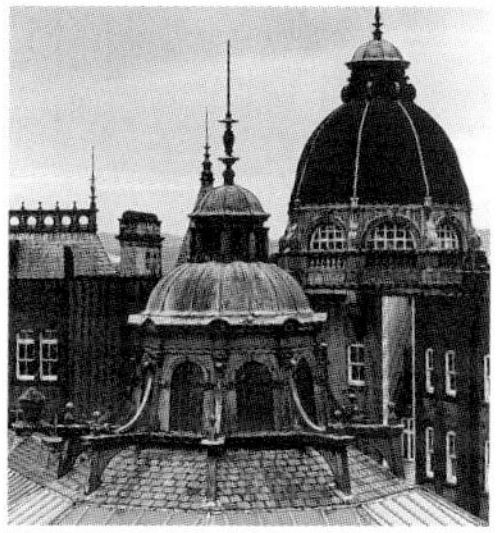

View of the market roof.

TEMPLE NEWSAM HOUSE

Built: 1488-1537 by Lord Darcy. & 1622-1630 by Sir Arthur Ingram. | Location: Temple Newsam Country Park.

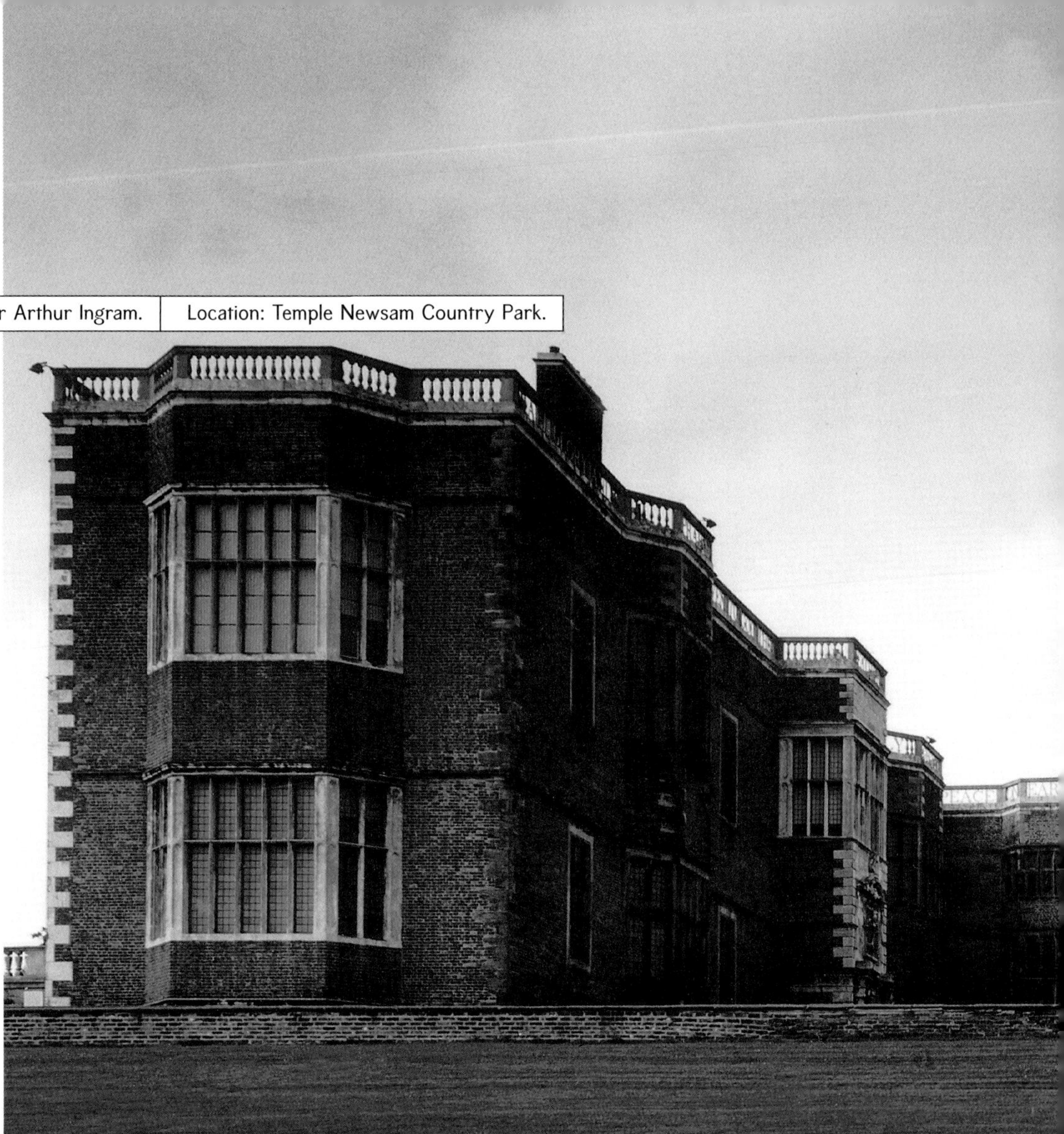

"My husband and I had our first real date at Temple Newsam House. The majestic building and the magnificent gardens, lakes and parkland along with my new found love, to me was the most beautiful place on earth. We returned the following year to see the rhododendrons in all their glory. It was like being part of a living painting. Temple Newsam was also the setting for our engagement, and we return every year to recall our memories. In turn our children and now our grandchildren have enjoyed the house and the parkland".

Patricia Wilson

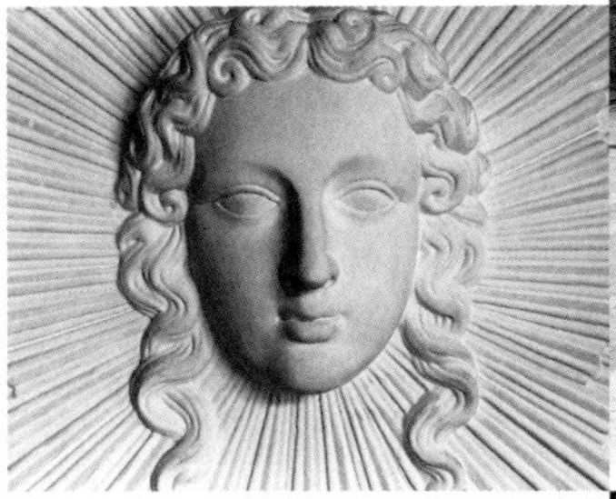

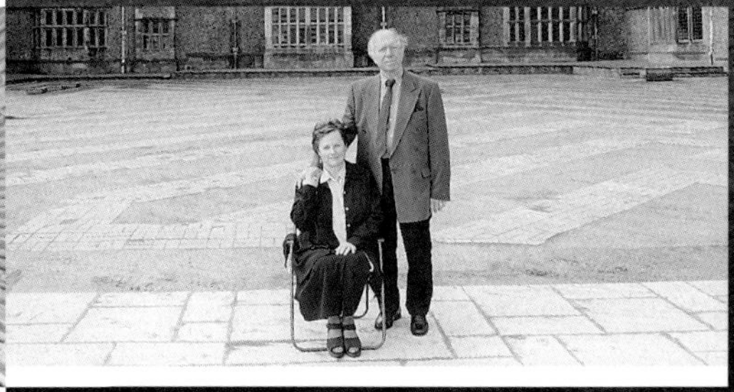

Detail of plaster work

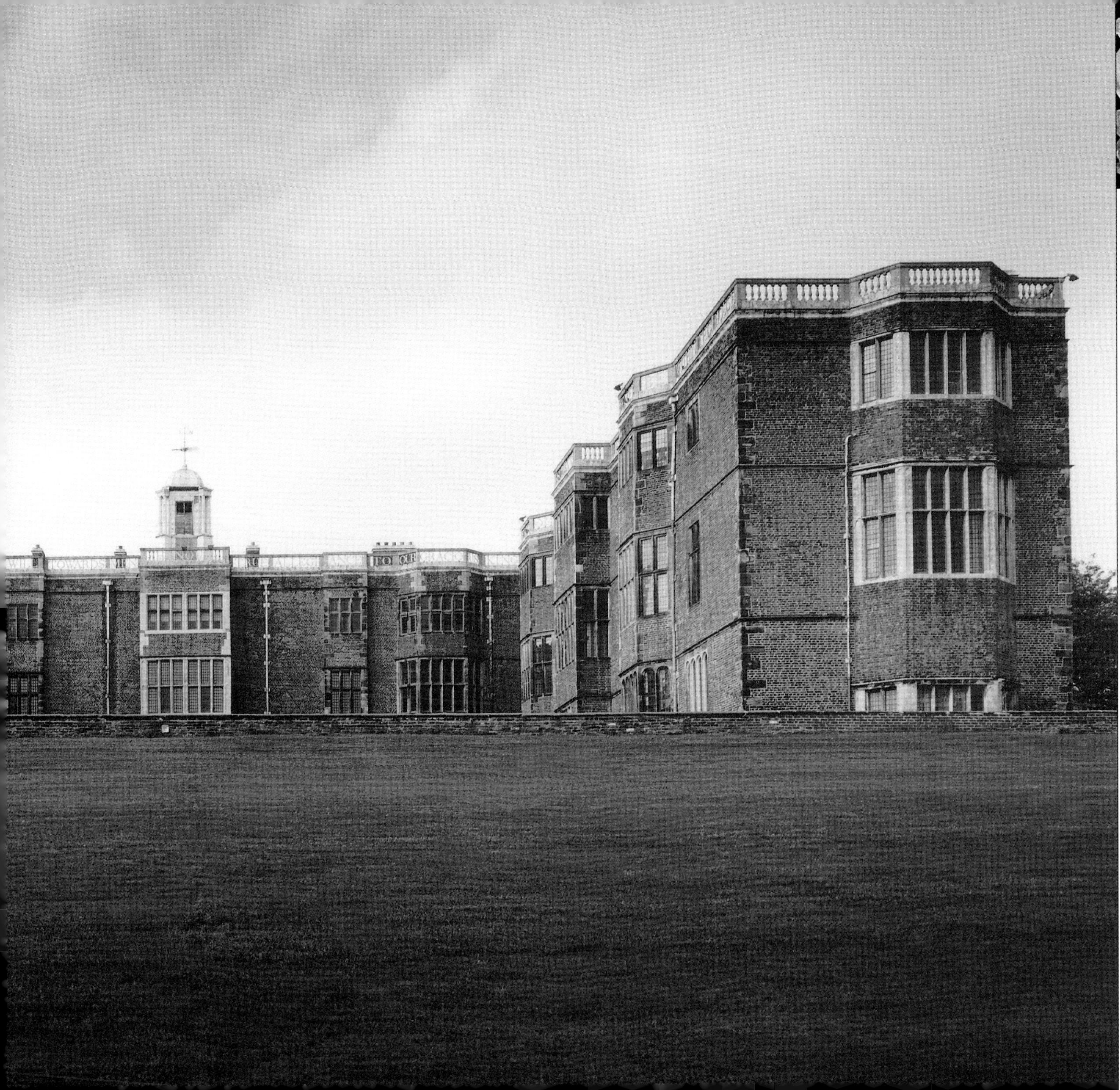

ALLOTMENTS

Location: Halton Moor Road, Cross Green.

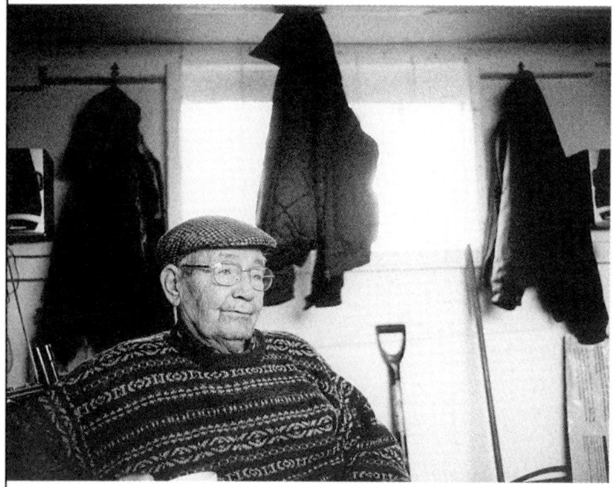

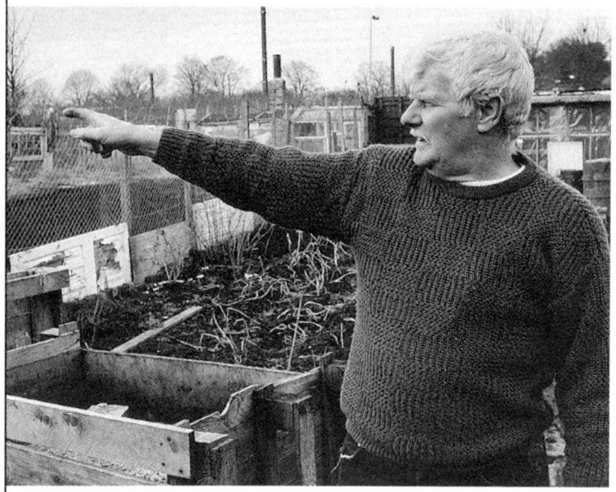

"Allotments, they are all going, loads of them, sold for building land. The contractors even get a good price for the top soil, its good stuff its been well looked after. Its great here, its an oasis, it helps me to get away from it all. There's loads of wildlife, newts, frogs, toads, and hedgehogs, its safe for them here. The songbirds are going, its the magpies and feral cats, they are the real pests. Magpies go from nest to nest destroying everything, if they don't kill them, the cats will. Its a real shame people don't realise what damage they cause. We're truly organic here, stuff tastes fantastic when you've grown it yourself. It makes you laugh when you see blokes going home with two carrier bags full and you know they haven't grown owt. We don't mind if they are feeding their families, we always grow too much. What does hurt is when your allotment gets wrecked by vandals who just destroy everything!".

Roger Mountain (bottom left)

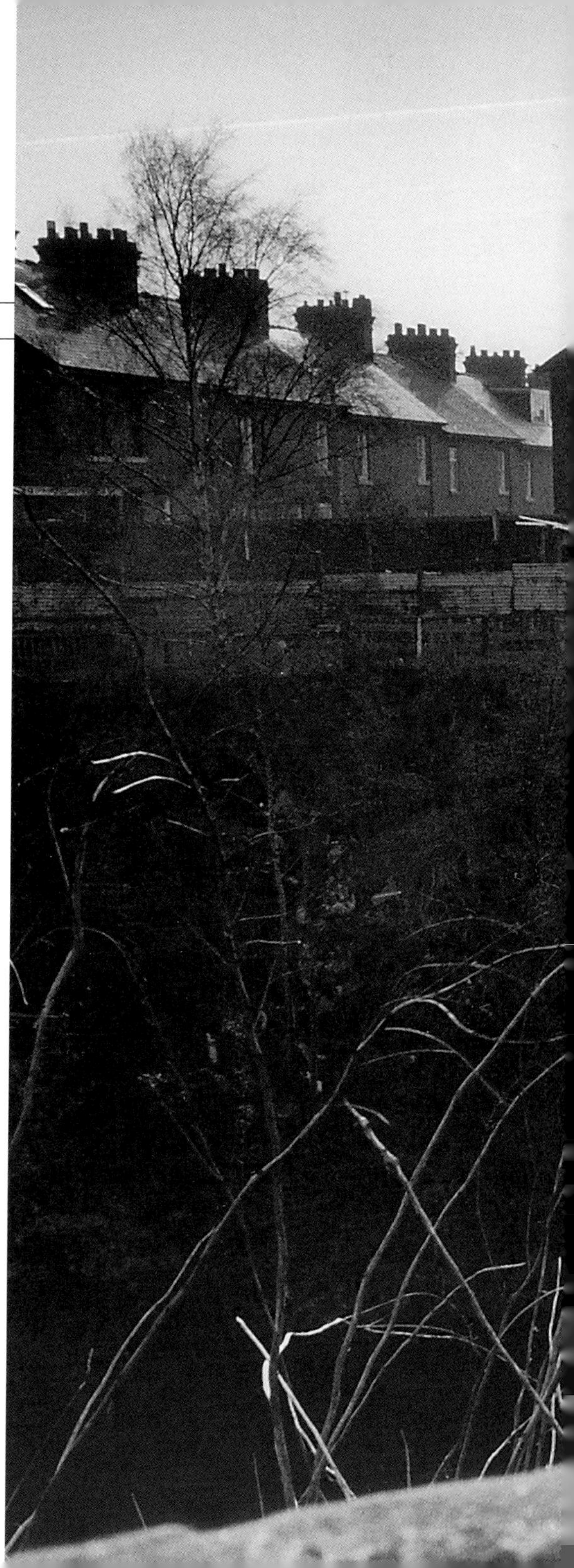

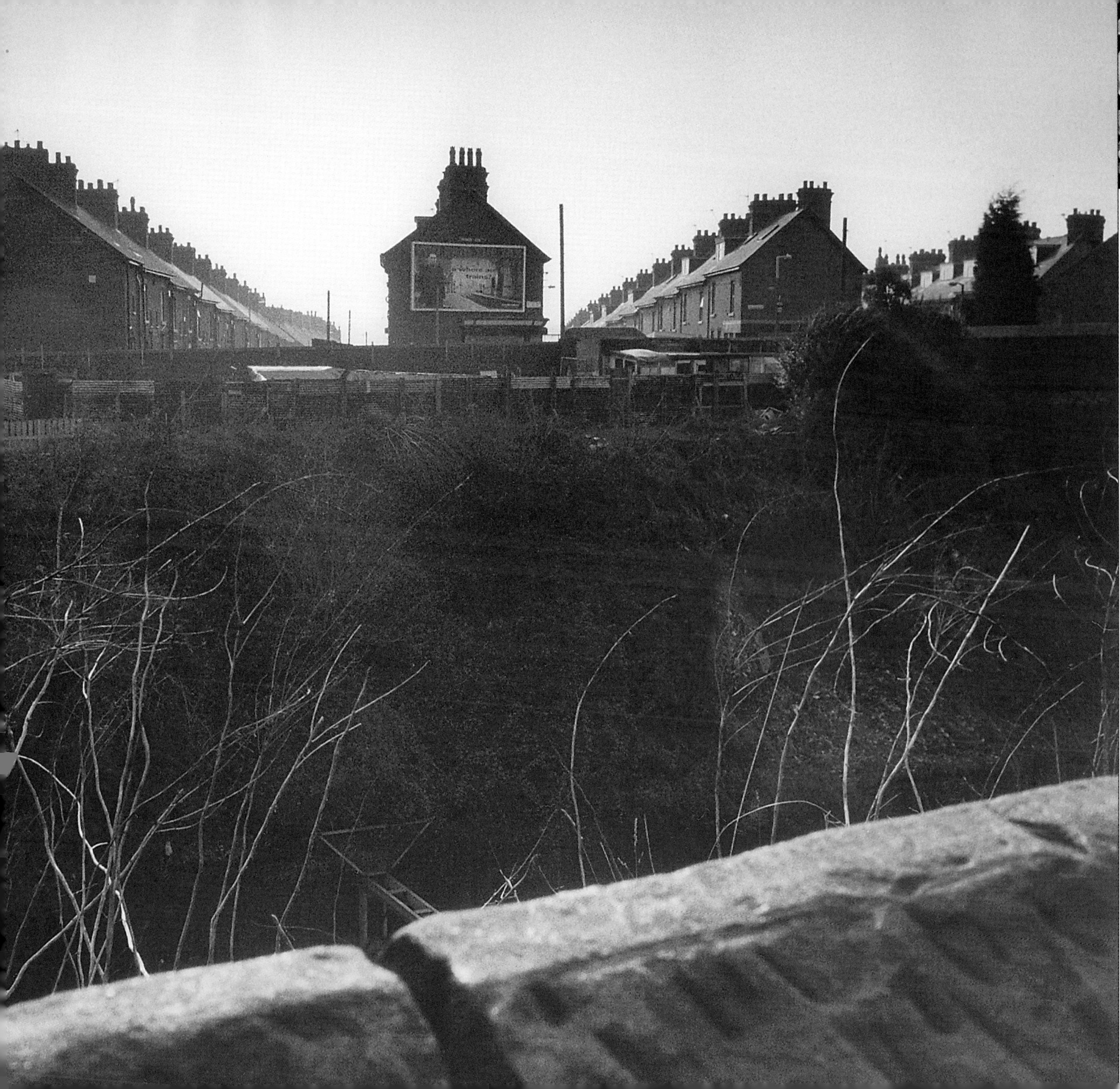

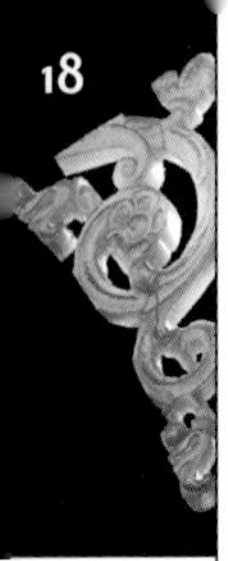

THE DOLPHIN PUB

Built: 1903.	Location: Vicar Lane.

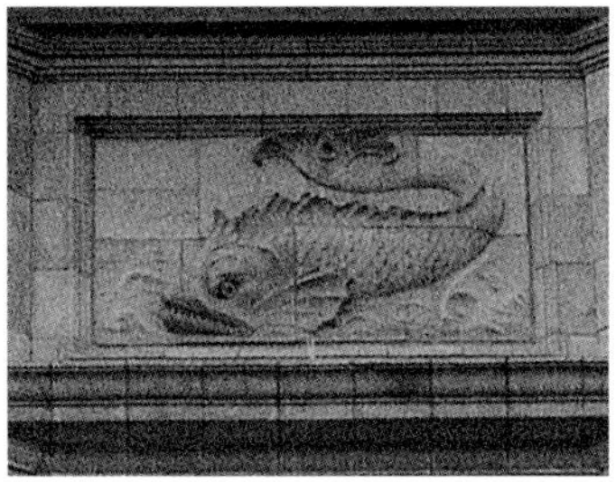

Dolphin detail from the facade of the Dolphin Pub.

"If you stand at the bus stop opposite and look up, there is a really nice dolphin at the top of the building, I really like that dolphin. My dad used to point it out to me when I was a kid and we were waiting at the bus stop. I bet there's not many people know its there, I do and it cheers me up when I see it".

Chris Howard

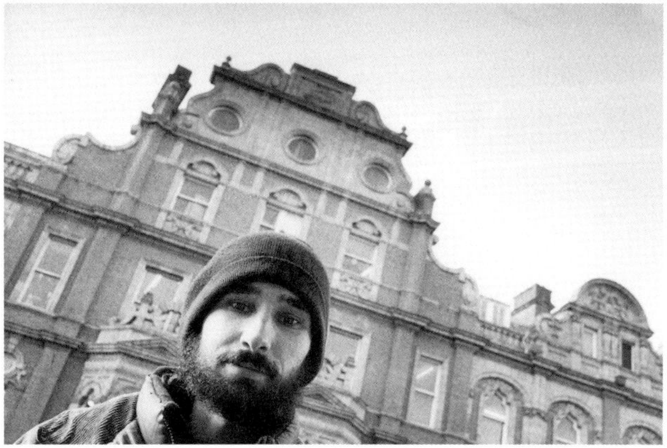

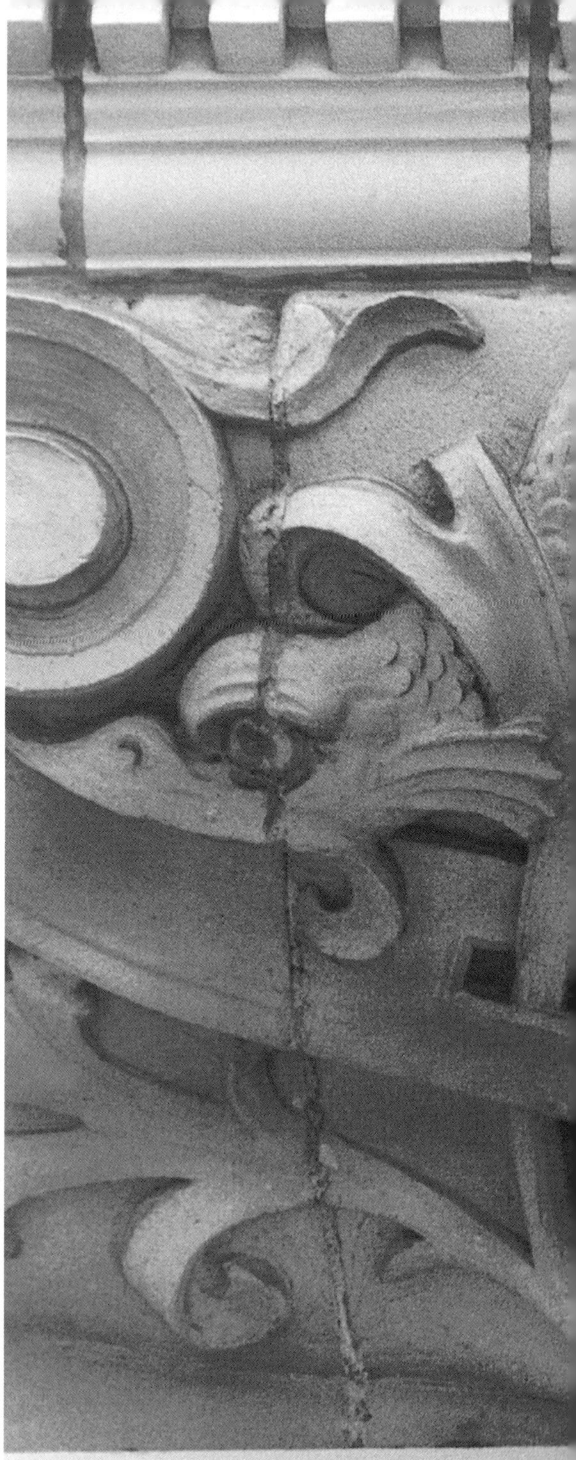

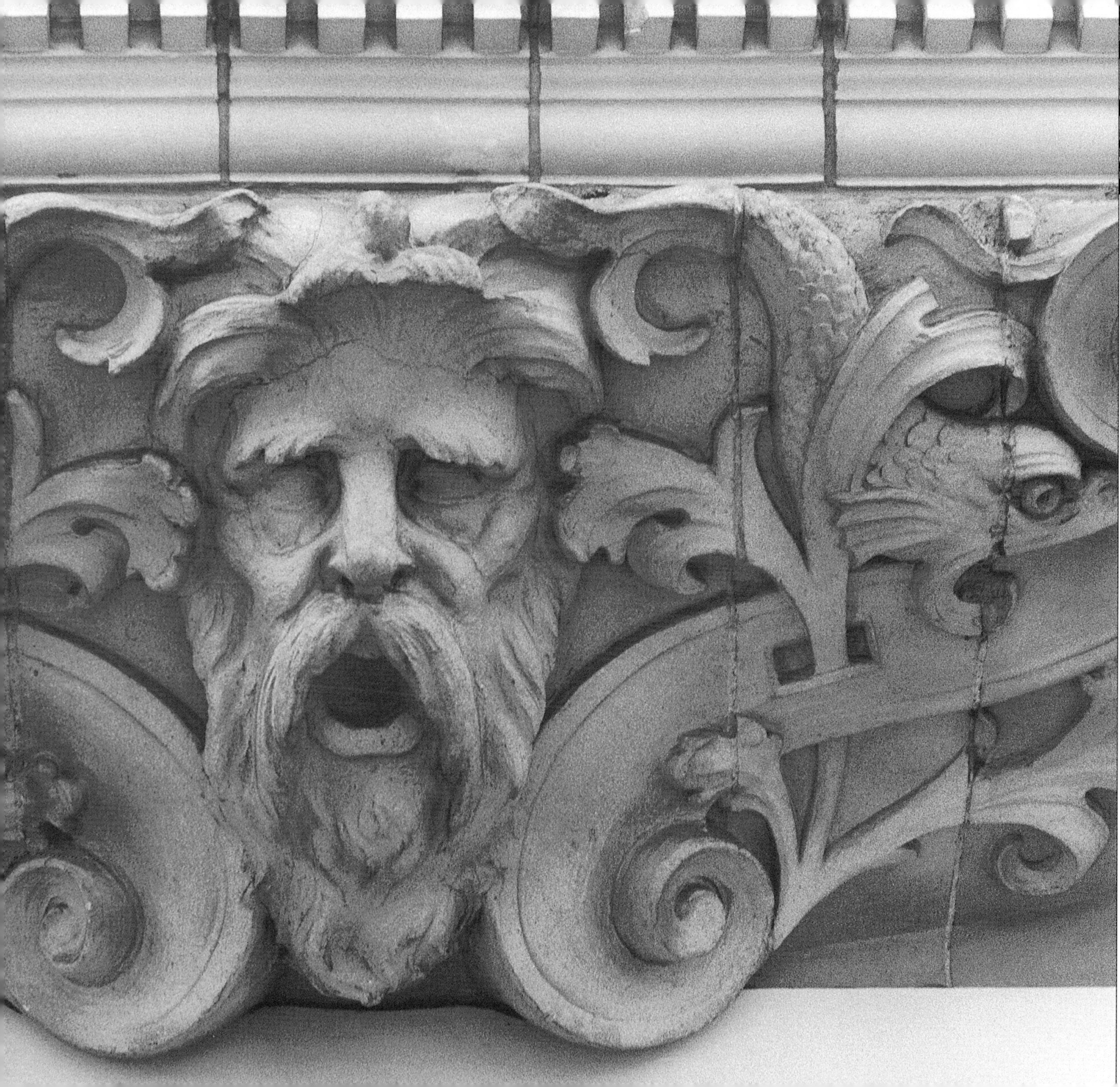

REFLECTIONS

Built: 1990's	Location: Leeds Shopping Plaza, Bond Street.

"I like buildings that have details like gargoyles and lions. Lots of detail, not like those modern 90 degree all square plastic buildings. I like to look at what's in front of me and see all the work and pride that's gone into it. Buildings that will last for a long time not fall down in a year or two".

Richard Gibson

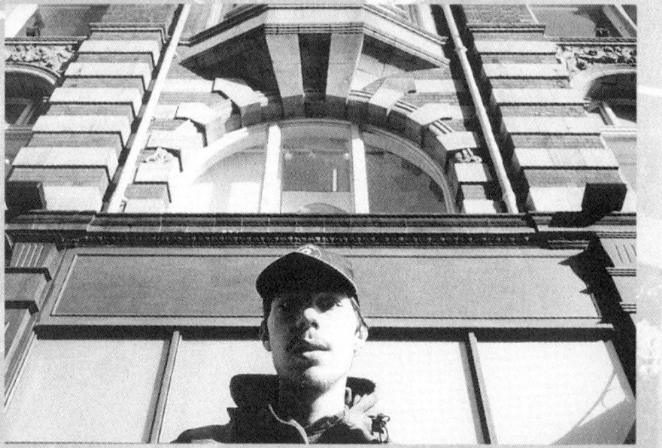

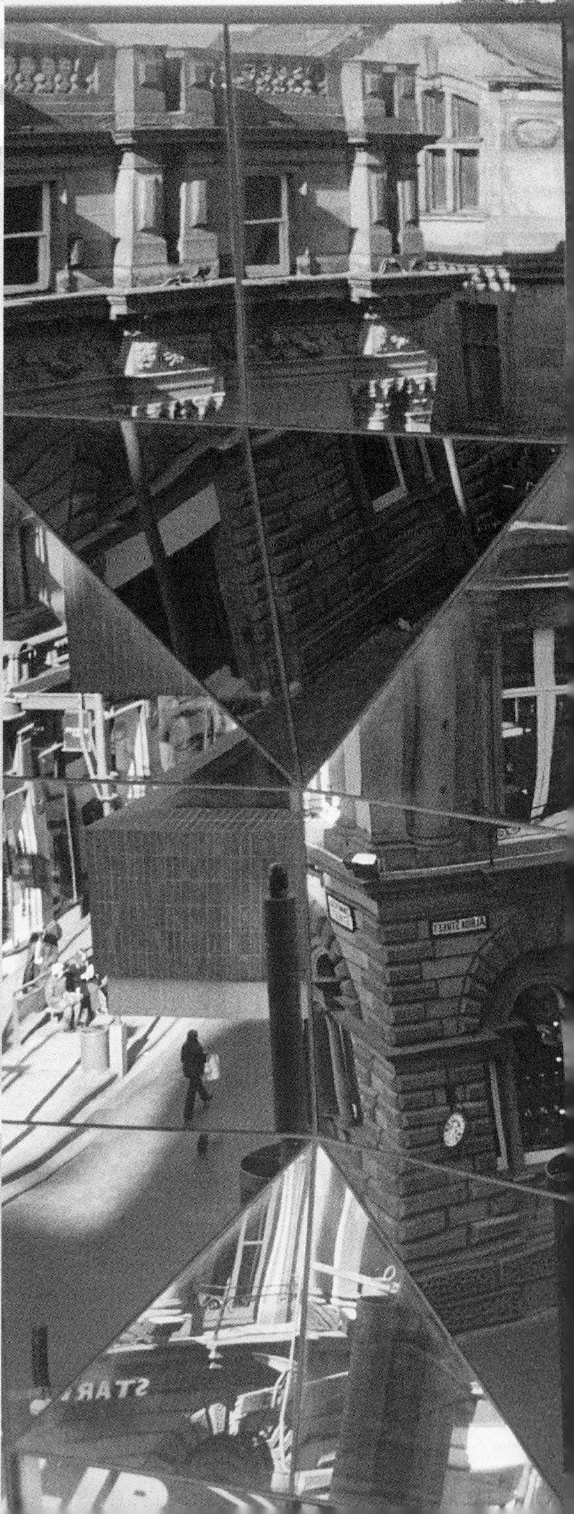

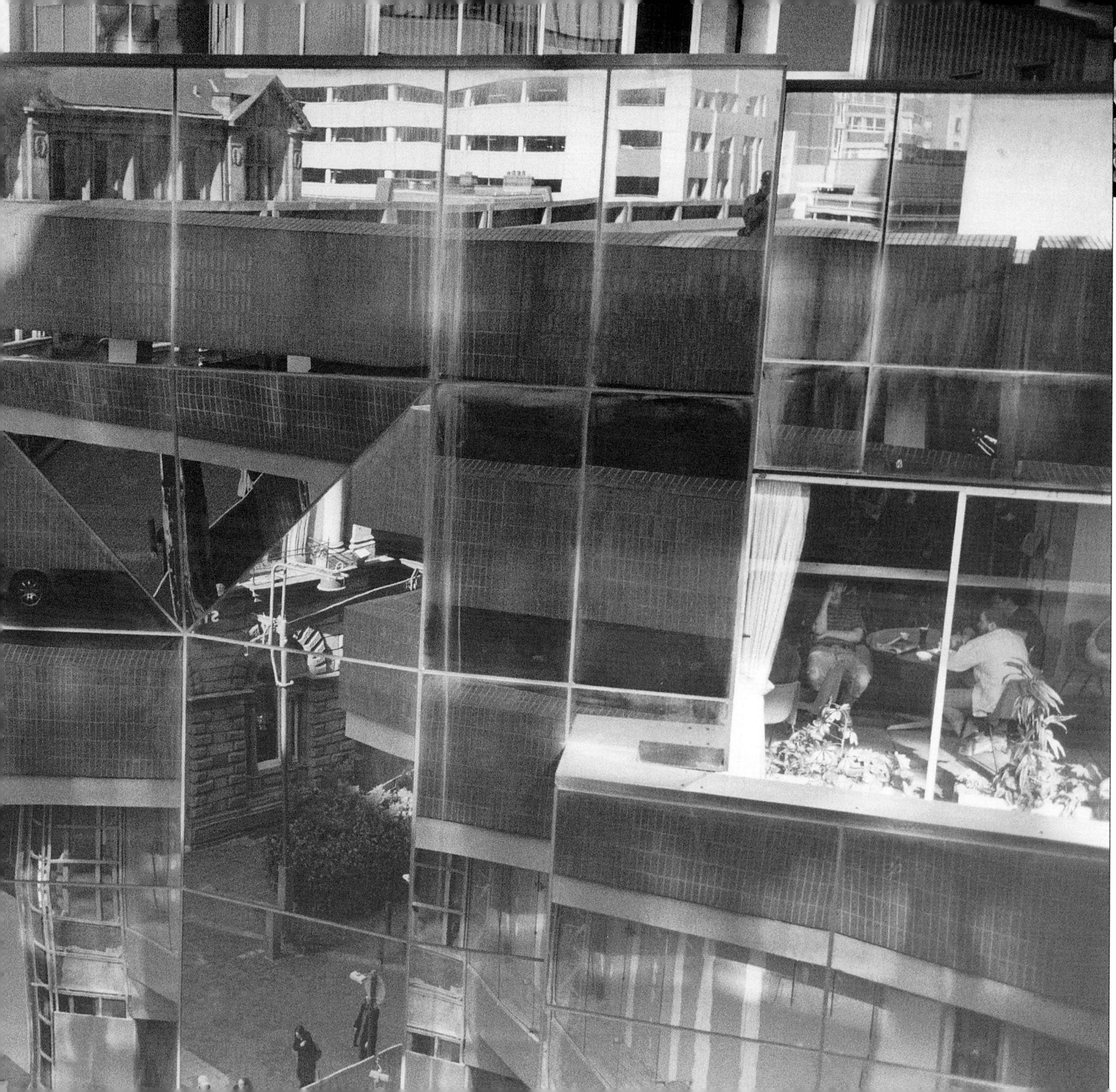

7TH AIREDALE SCOUT AND GUIDE HEADQUARTERS

Built: 1930's.	Location: New Road, Horsforth.

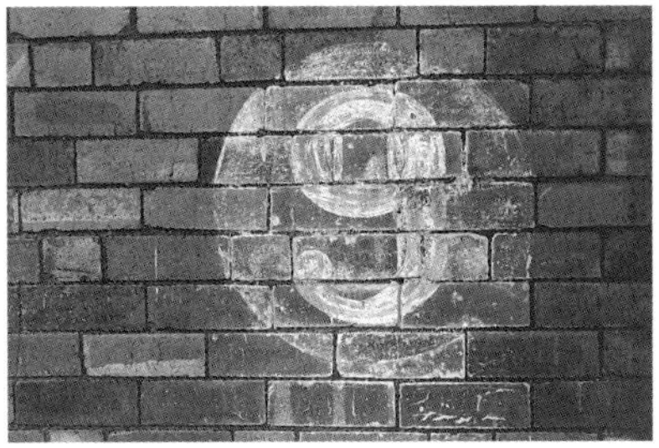

Detail of wall from the Hunters Greave Scout Hut.

"Airedale Scouts, the 9th Airedale that's who we were, I don't think it exists anymore. I joined in 1935, I was 8 years old, we met in Horsforth in the Scout hut on the main road. After the War Mr. Greaves gave the Scouts some land near Bramley Falls woods, it had been an ammunition factory. We would walk down the Cuckoo steps in Horsforth over the Railway bridge and along the path. The camp was between the canal and the river. We built a hut there on a concrete base, inside was an old stove, where we could dry clothes etc, if they got wet. I loved camping, it was well used Hunters Greave, there was no Warden, it was open air, open to the River Aire as well, loved it, I hope its still there!"

Alan Boyes

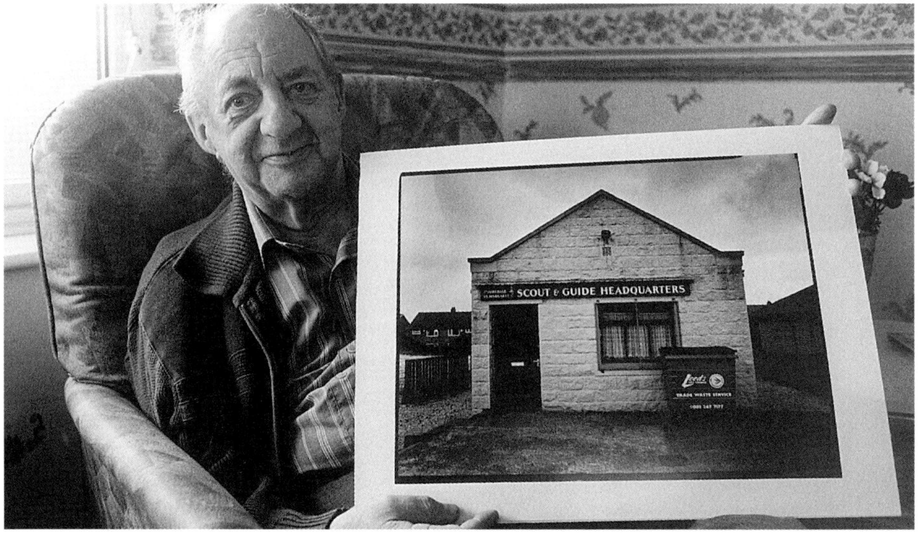

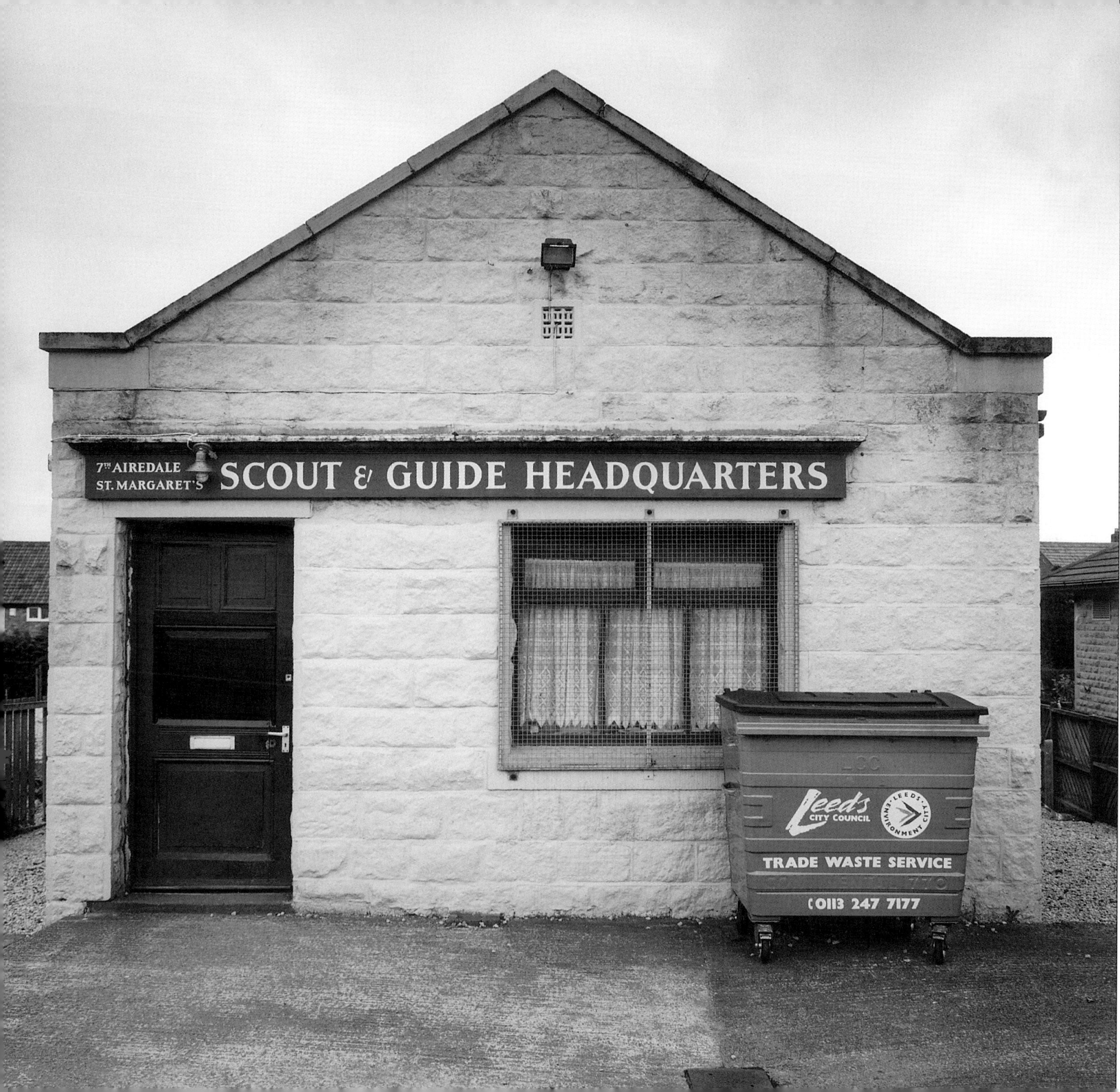
7TH AIREDALE
ST. MARGARET'S
SCOUT & GUIDE HEADQUARTERS
Leeds
CITY COUNCIL
LEEDS ENVIRONMENT CITY
TRADE WASTE SERVICE
0113 247 7177

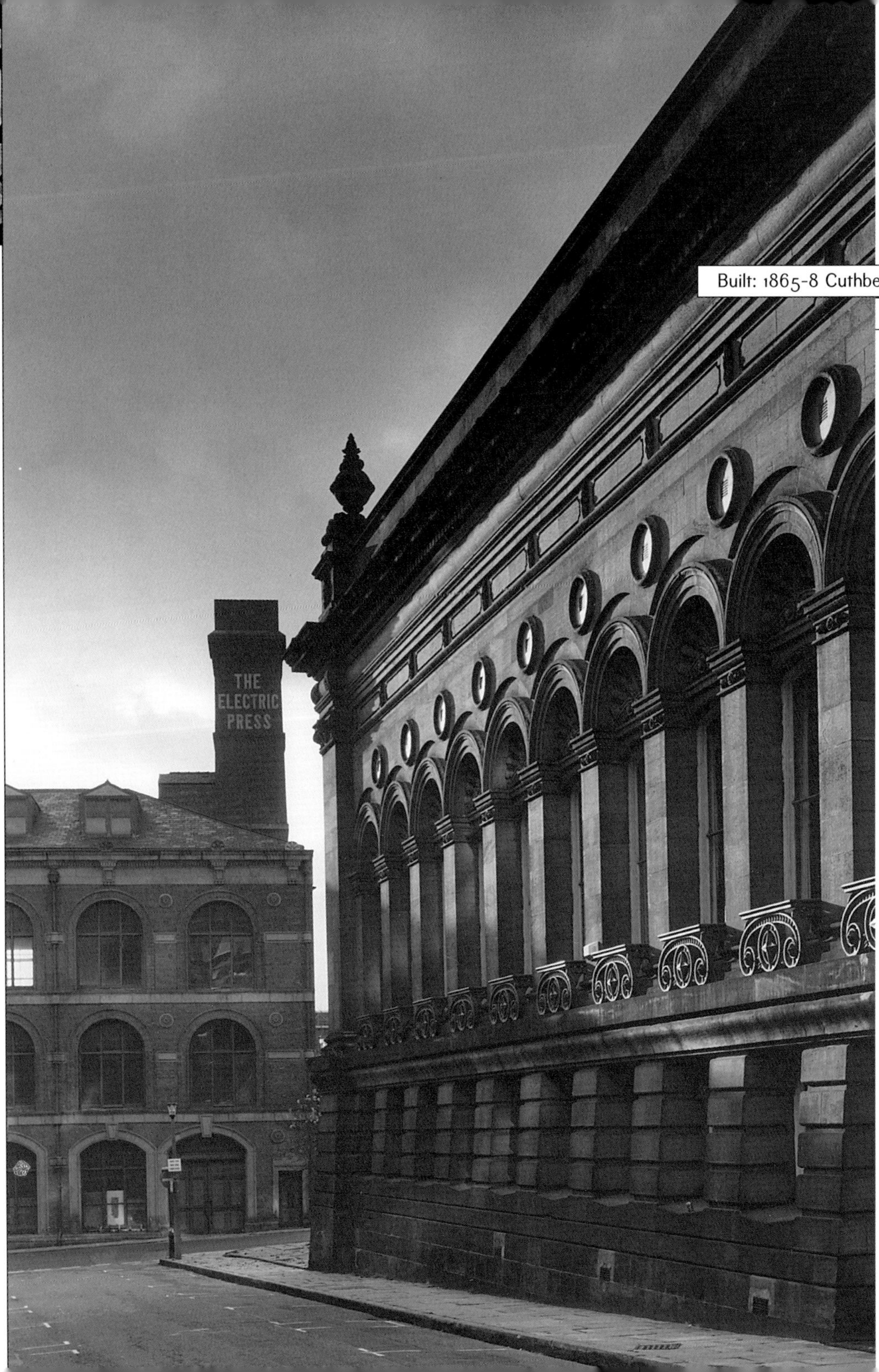

THE CIVIC THEATRE

Built: 1865-8 Cuthbert Brodrick. | Location: Cookridge Street.

Originally The Leeds Institute of Science and Art.

"Leeds must be unique among the great cities of Britain in not having a city centre showplace for its history or for its museum collections. The Yorkshire Archeological Society was therefore delighted to hear that a solution had been found - the conversion of the fine Cuthbert Brodrick Leeds Institute of Science and Arts into a new Leeds City Museum.

Peter Addyman,
President of the Yorkshire Archeological Society

"I think the Civic Theatre would be better as a theatre than a museum - I'm attached to the Civic Theatre because I saw Dear Octopus there as a boy, Toad of Toad Hall and lots of pantomimes, many of them starring Basil Sheldon who was a leading light of the amateurs then. So I hope it stays a theatre and I hope somewhere is found for a museum too"

Alan Bennett
Author and Screen writer
Yorkshire Post Friday 23 March 2001

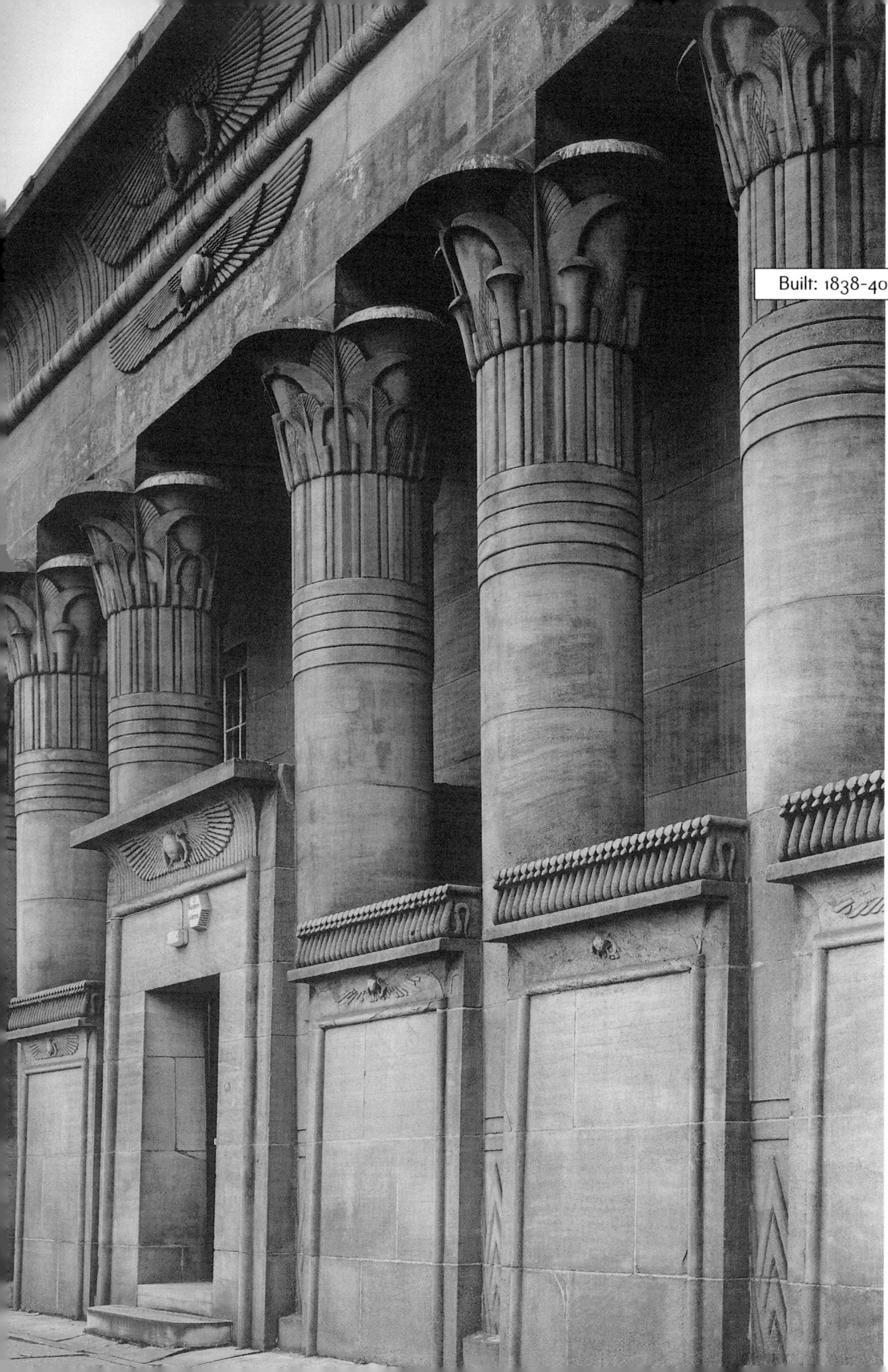

MARSHALL'S TEMPLE MILL

Built: 1838-40 Ignatius Bonomi.	Location: Marshall Street, Holbeck.

"I can remember going to Leeds with my father, when I was quite young. He told me we were going to see an egyptian temple and some chinese dragons. I remember being excited and a little scared. When we walked into Marshall Street, I couldn't understand why this strange building had ended up in the back streets of Leeds and I was worried that we shouldn't have been there looking at it.

It seemed a very sinister place, in the failing light of a winters afternoon. I was glad when we made our way to the bustling market for some sweets and a drink and a look at the bright red chinese dragons that decorate the hall".

Ian Beesley

ST. PETERS - LEEDS PARISH CHURCH

Built: 1837-41 R. Dennis Chantrell.	Location: Kirkgate.

" It reminds me of happier days, when I was young I sung in Rothwell Church Choir and when I was 11 we came to the Parish Church for a music festival. On the third day we sang on Radio Leeds"

David Braithwaite

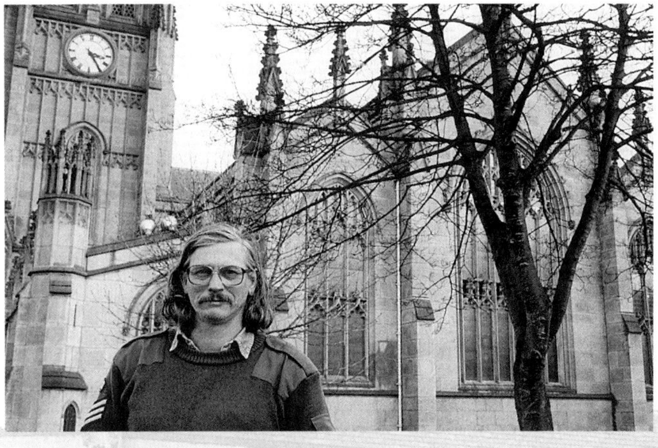

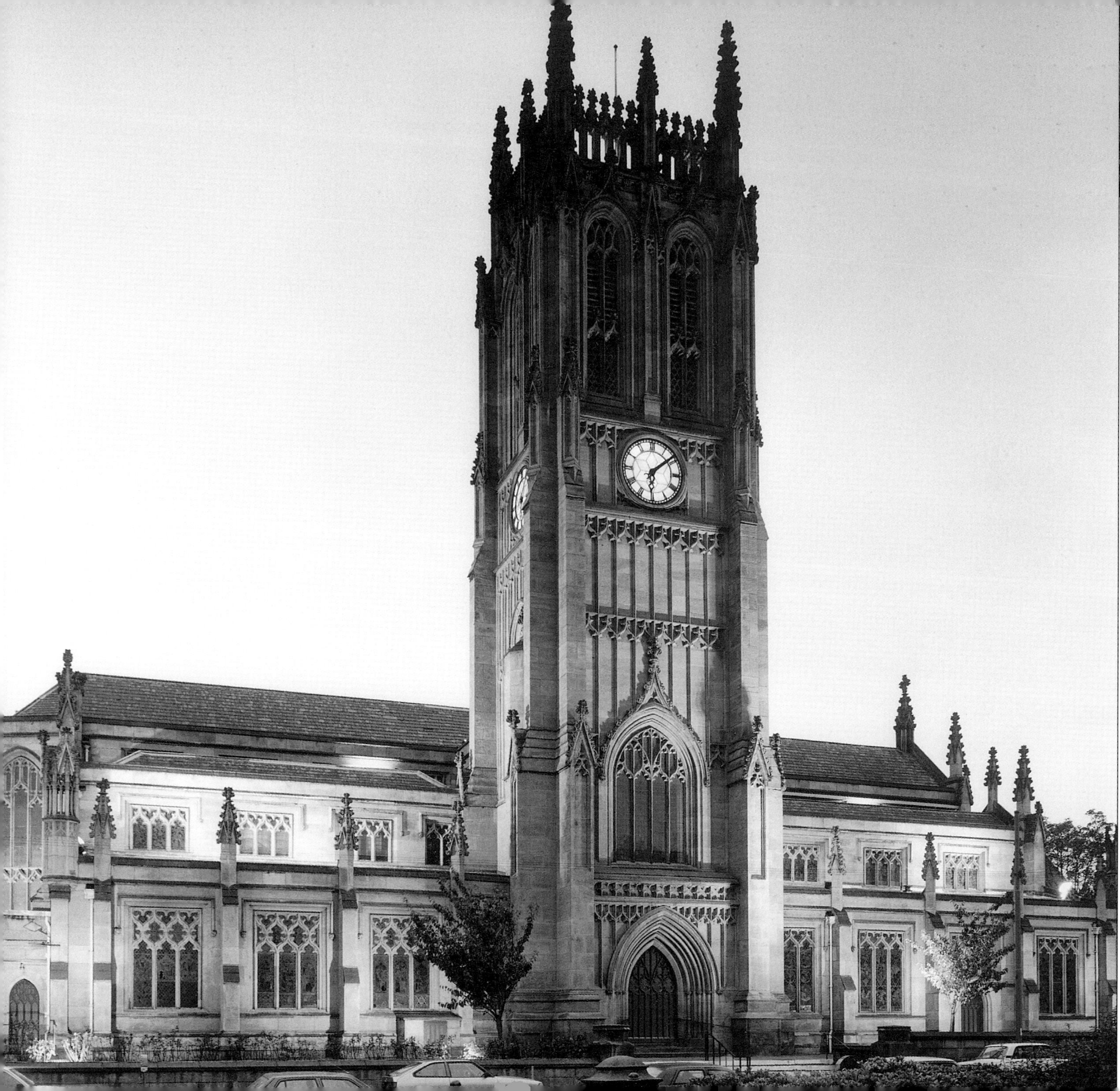

THORESBY SCHOOL

Built: 1900 W.S. Braithwaite.	Location: Great George Street.

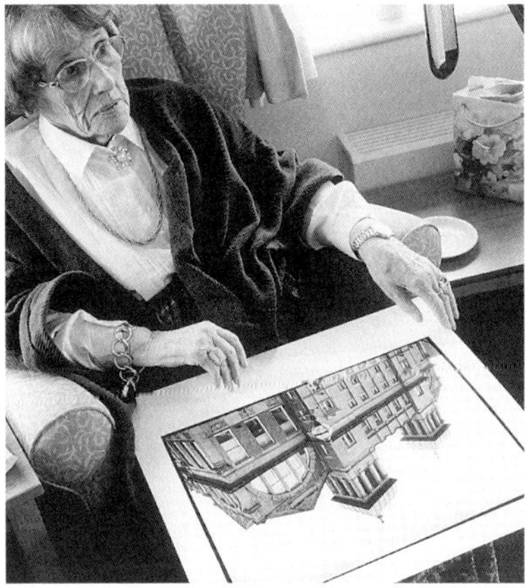

"I went to Thoresby School, George Street from 1926 to 1931. The fees were 9 guineas a term, which was a lot of money in those days. It was a girls only school, the boys school was opposite. We were kept strictly apart. We had different starting and finishing times. We finished at 4 pm and the boys finished at 3.45 pm. Even the playgrounds were separate! Ours was at street level and the boys was on the roof.

I can remember the assembly hall, it was all tiled with lovely wrought iron railings. The headmistress's study overlooked the hall so she could keep an eye on you. For punishment she used to make you take her dog for a walk, I loved dogs so it wasn't much of a punishment for me!"

Mary Graham

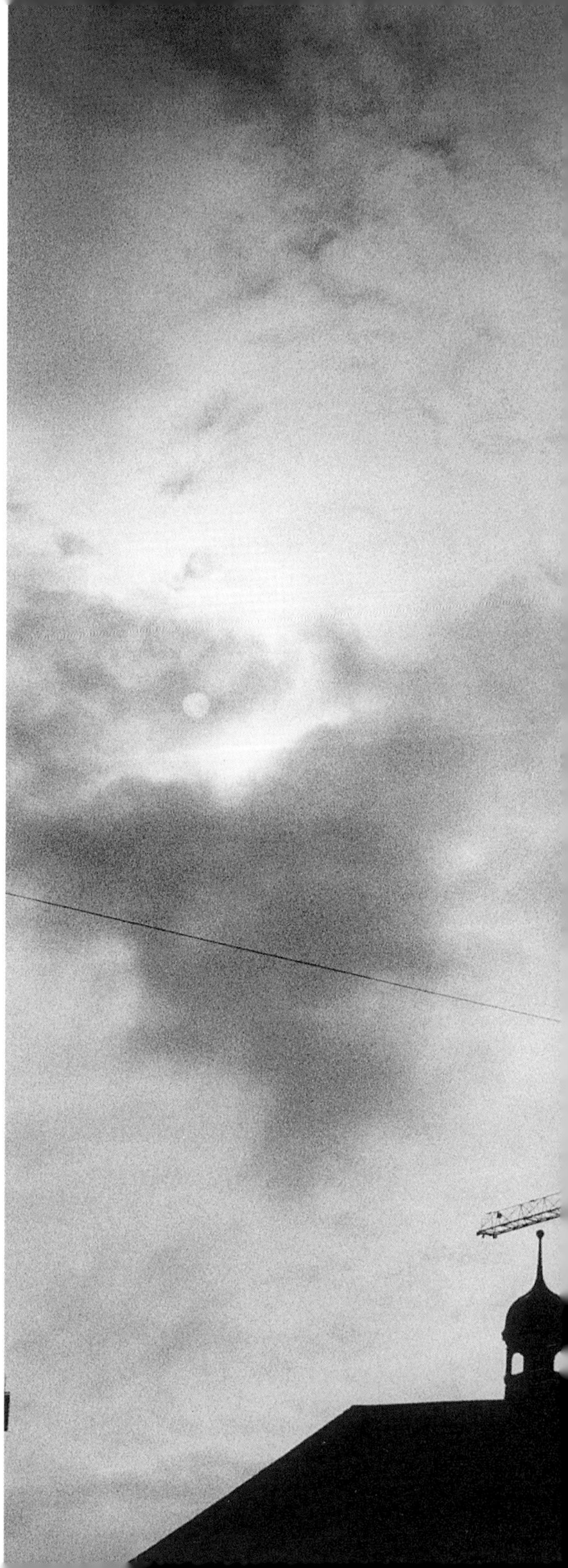

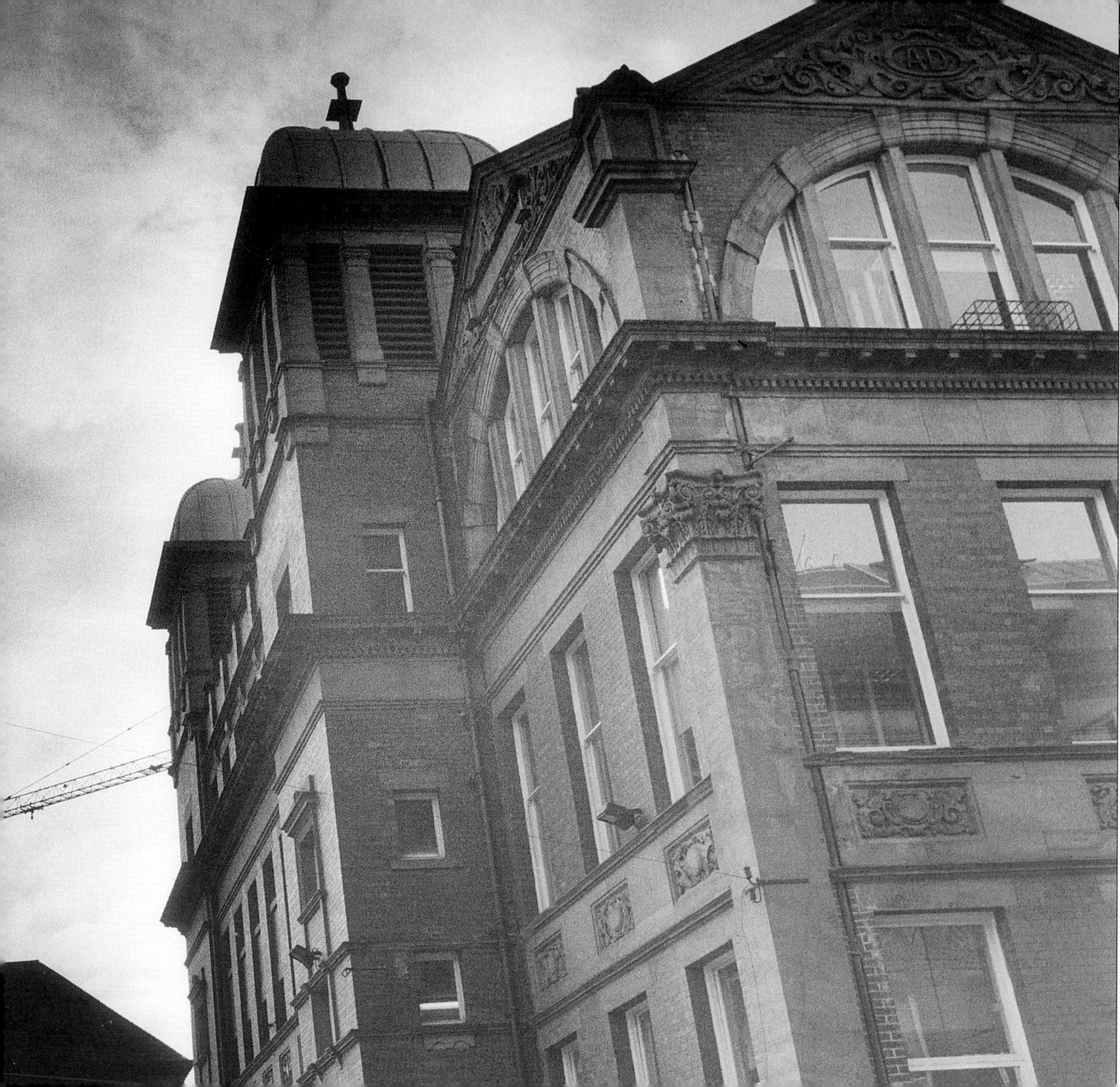

THE TOWN HALL

Built: 1853-8 Cuthbert Brodrick. | Location: Victoria Square, the Headrow.

" The Town Hall steps was my home for 3 weeks, it's very sheltered up behind those columns and when the lights go out at 11 pm, nobody knows you are there, so there's no trouble. We'd be up and away before 8 am. We had to stop sleeping there because of the Piano Concert, but the staff were really polite. Yeah it was a good place".

Robert Crompton

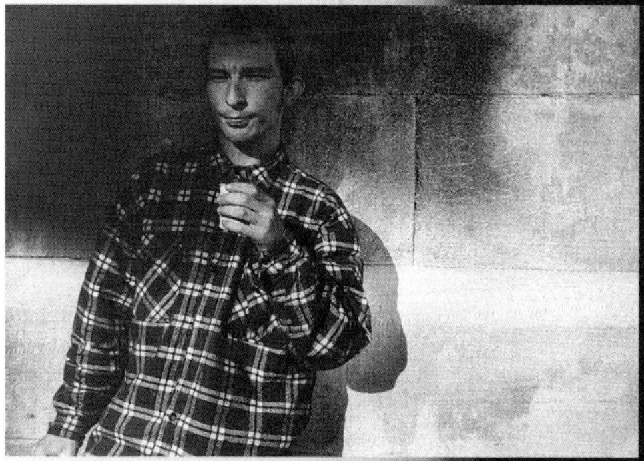

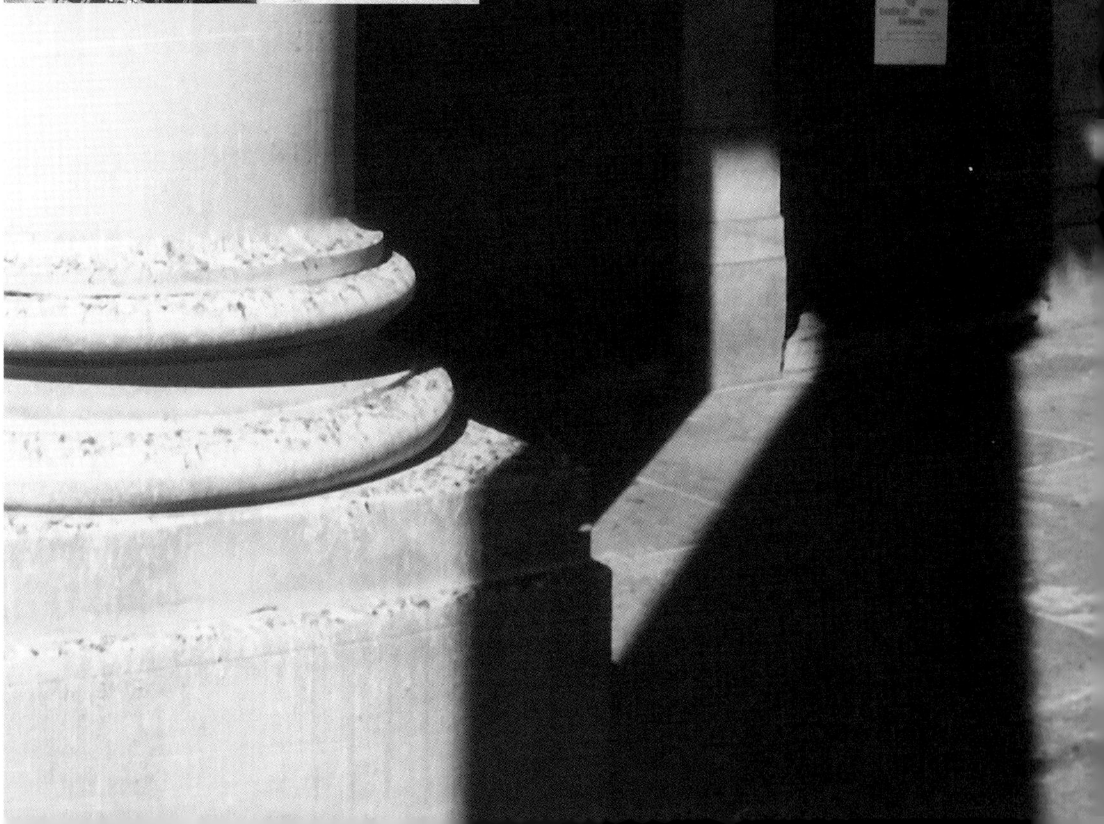

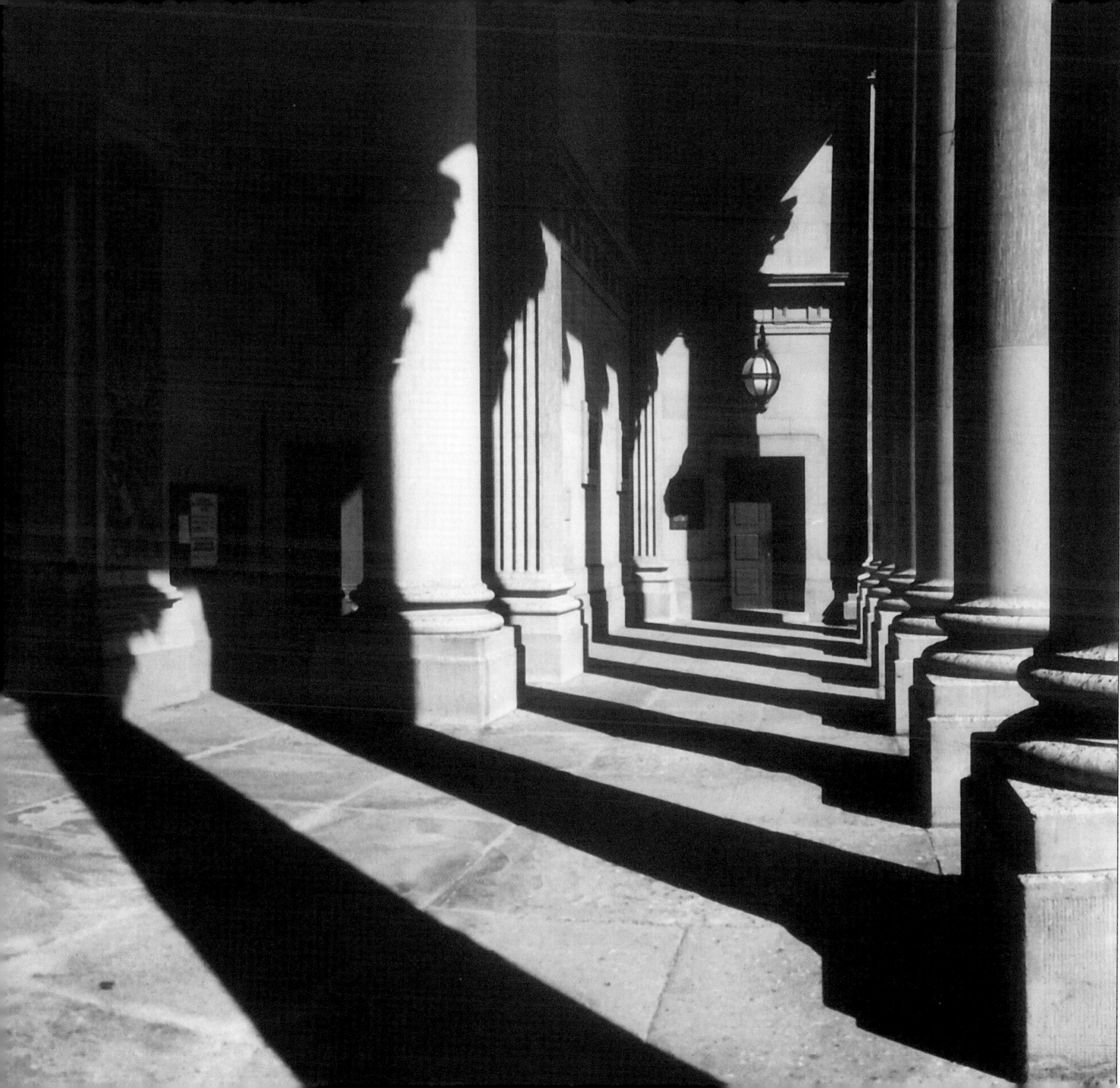

125 JACK LANE

Built: 1881.	Location: Hunslet.

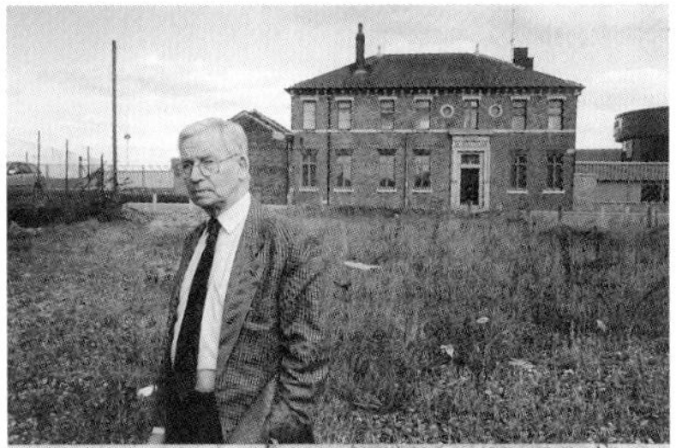

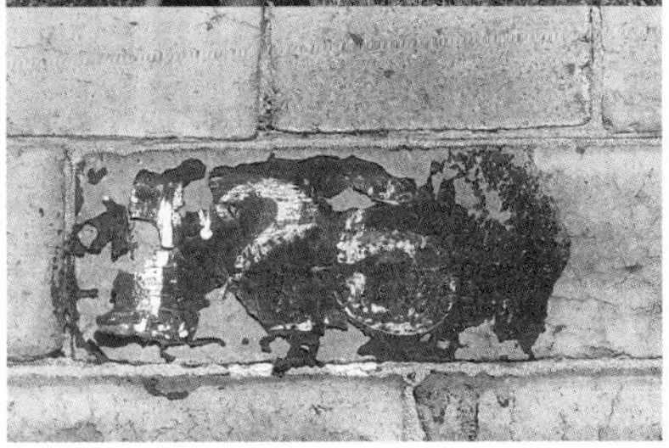

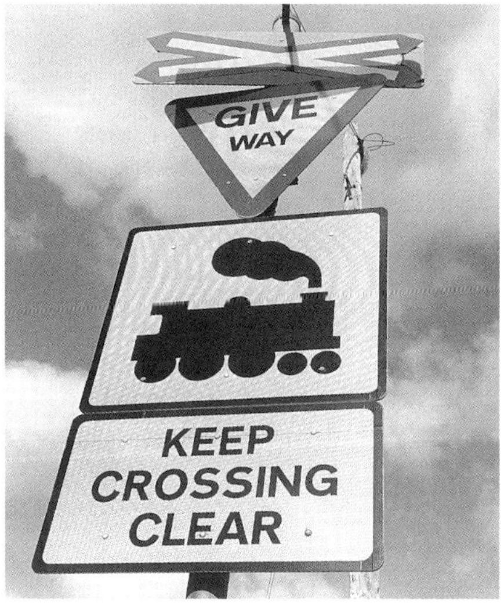

"125 Jack Lane has played such an significant role in many lives, not least my own. This building not only provided a livelihood for thousands of people for over a century, but its products have been instrumental in shaping the fortunes of others from almost every walk of life throughout the world. The most poignant memories I have are the first and the last. Firstly waiting at the office window on my first day at work, 7.52 am on August 2nd 1949 and being greeted by the sight of a steam locomotive crashing through Hudswell Clarkes's wall opposite and out into Jack Lane amidst a shower of bricks and a cloud of dust - just as the starting hooter blew.

Lastly going back after the works had closed to find my former secretary as the sole occupant of the building disposing of the final paper work. Very sad!"

Donald Townsley

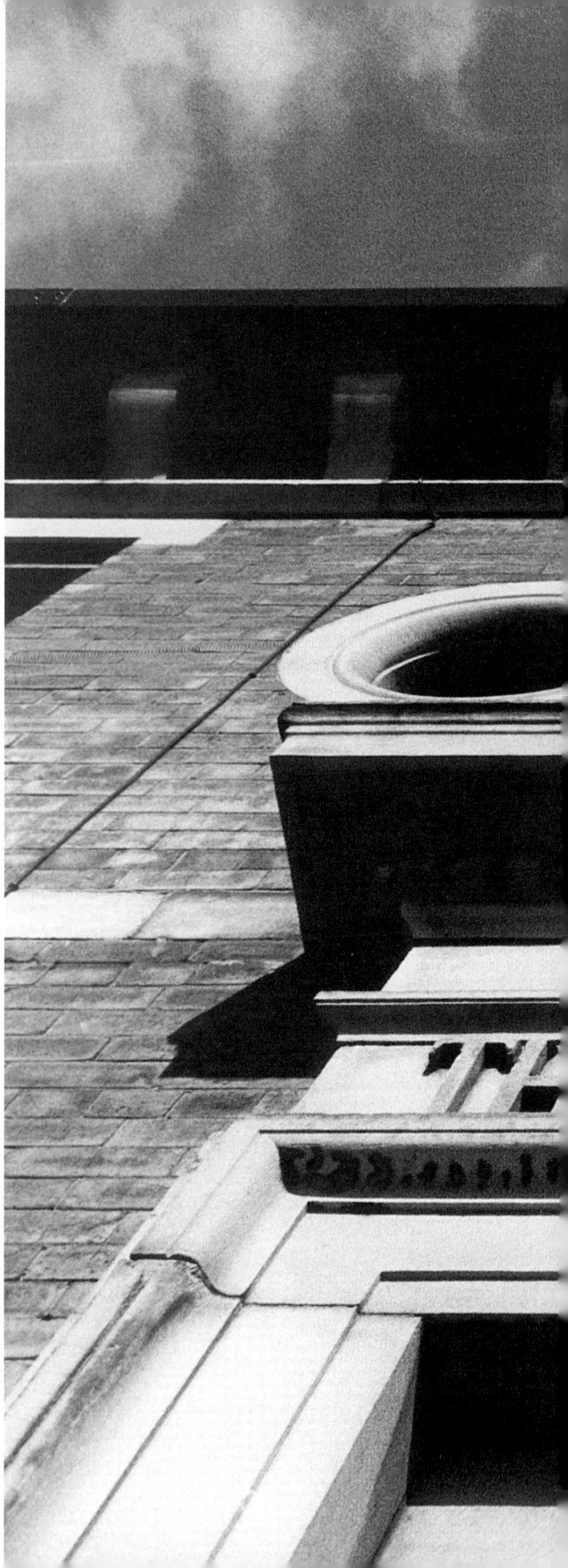

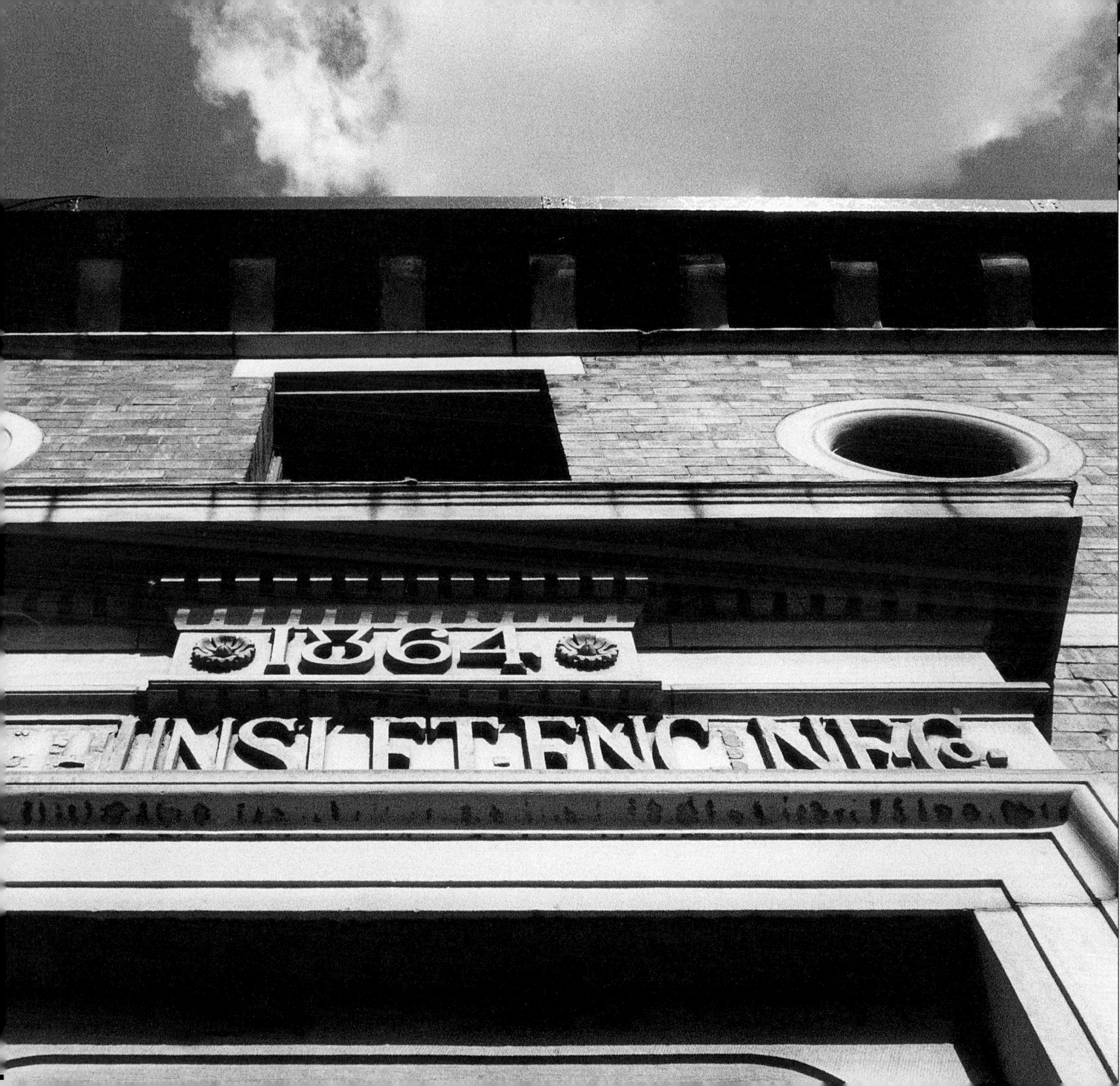
1864

STREETS

Built: 1896-1908 Joseph Pullan and Sons.	Location: The Nosters Beeston.

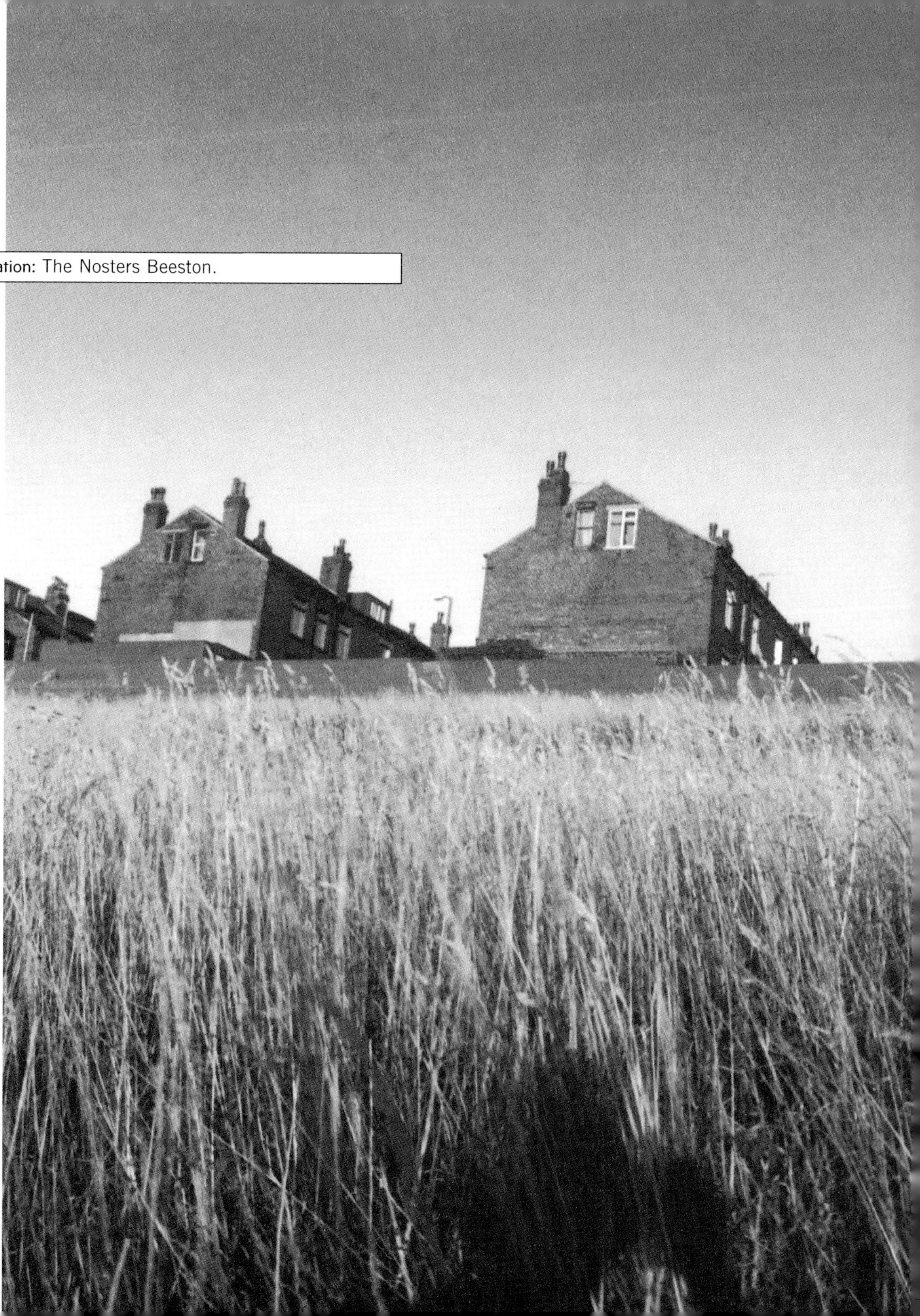

"I lived in Eastfield Street near the town centre, I remember that when our clock ran down, we used to go out into the street and check the local school clock".

Betty Barker

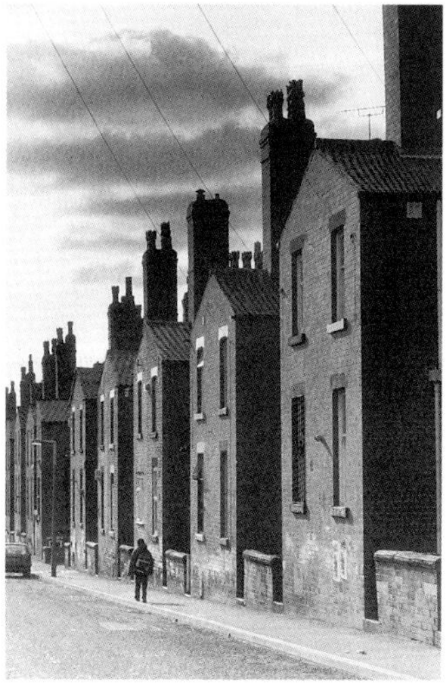

Back of Pearson Grove,
Hyde Park.
Built 1895-1900 probably
by Walmsley Brothers.

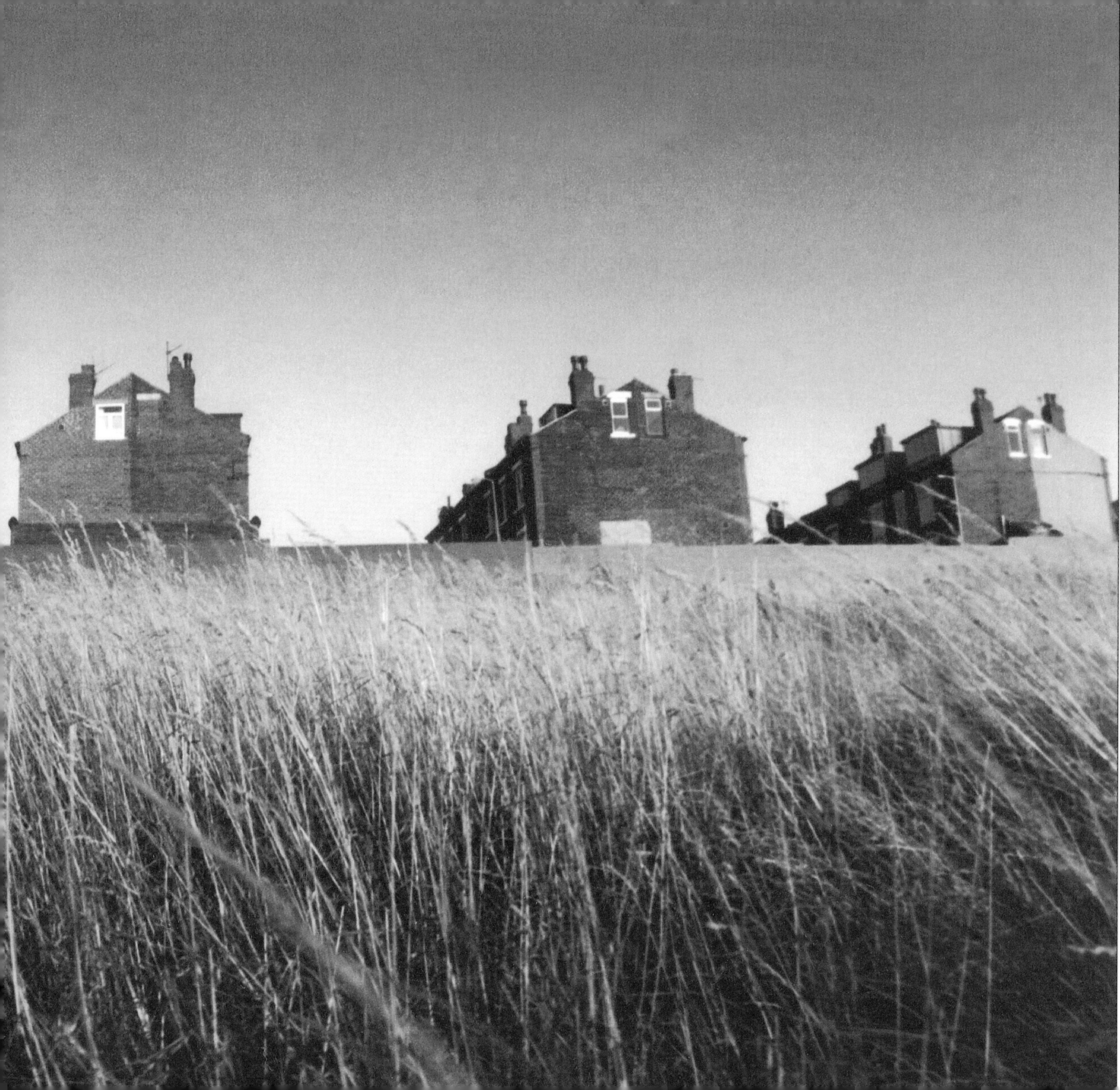

LEEDS UNITED FOOTBALL STADIUM

Location: Elland Road.

"Its becoming more like a theme park than a football ground".

Anonymous Leeds United Fan

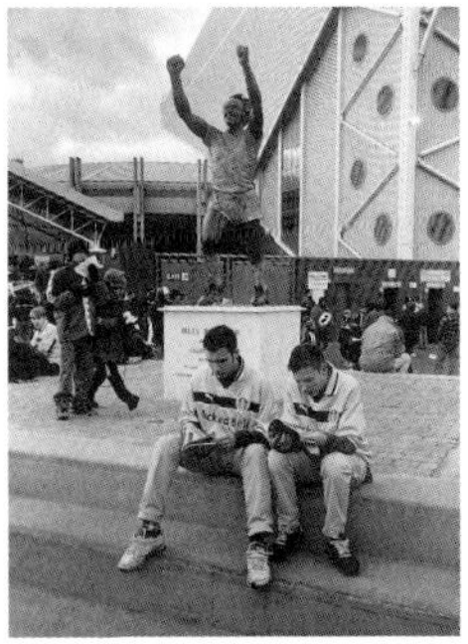

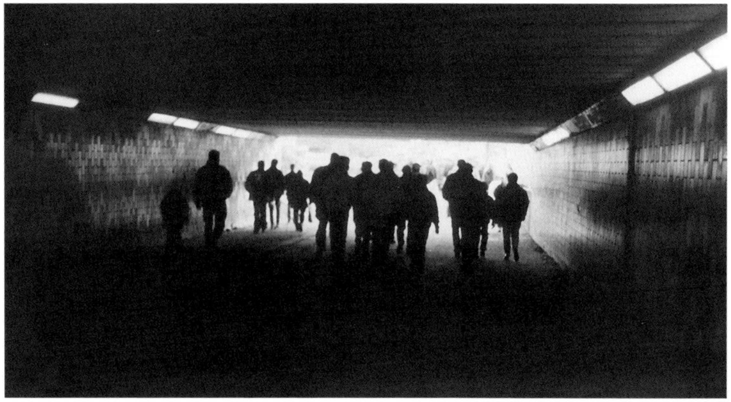

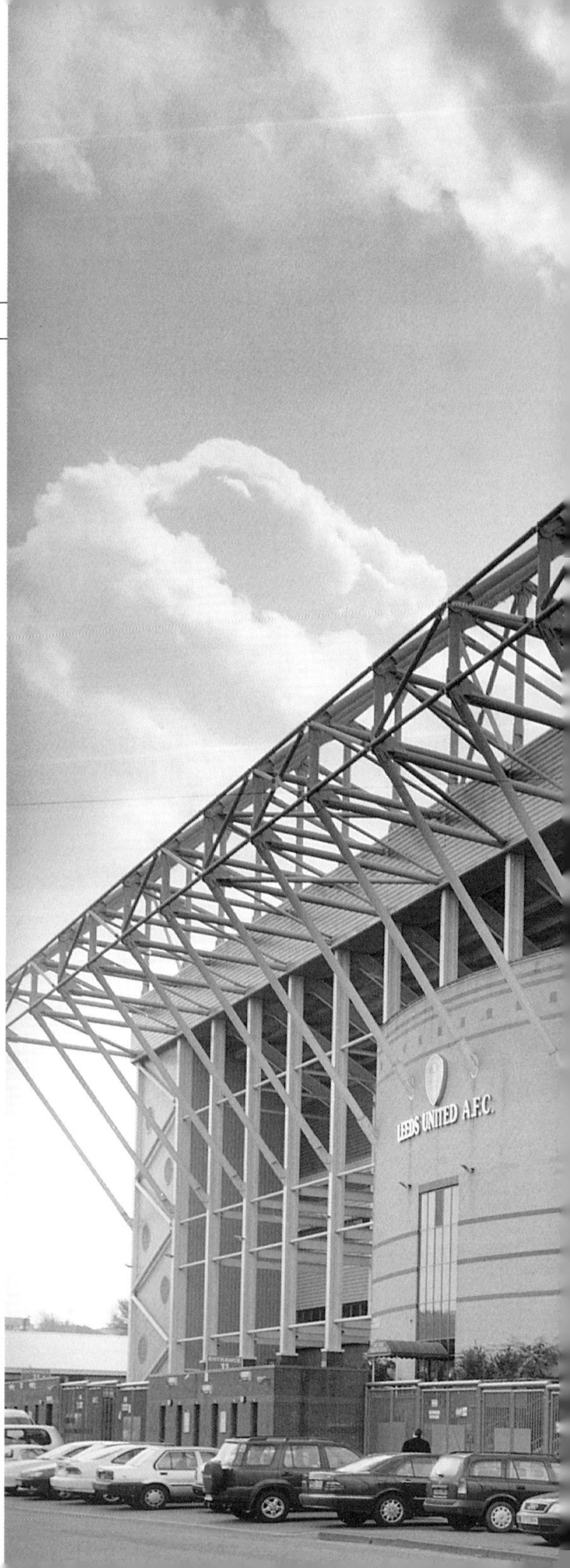

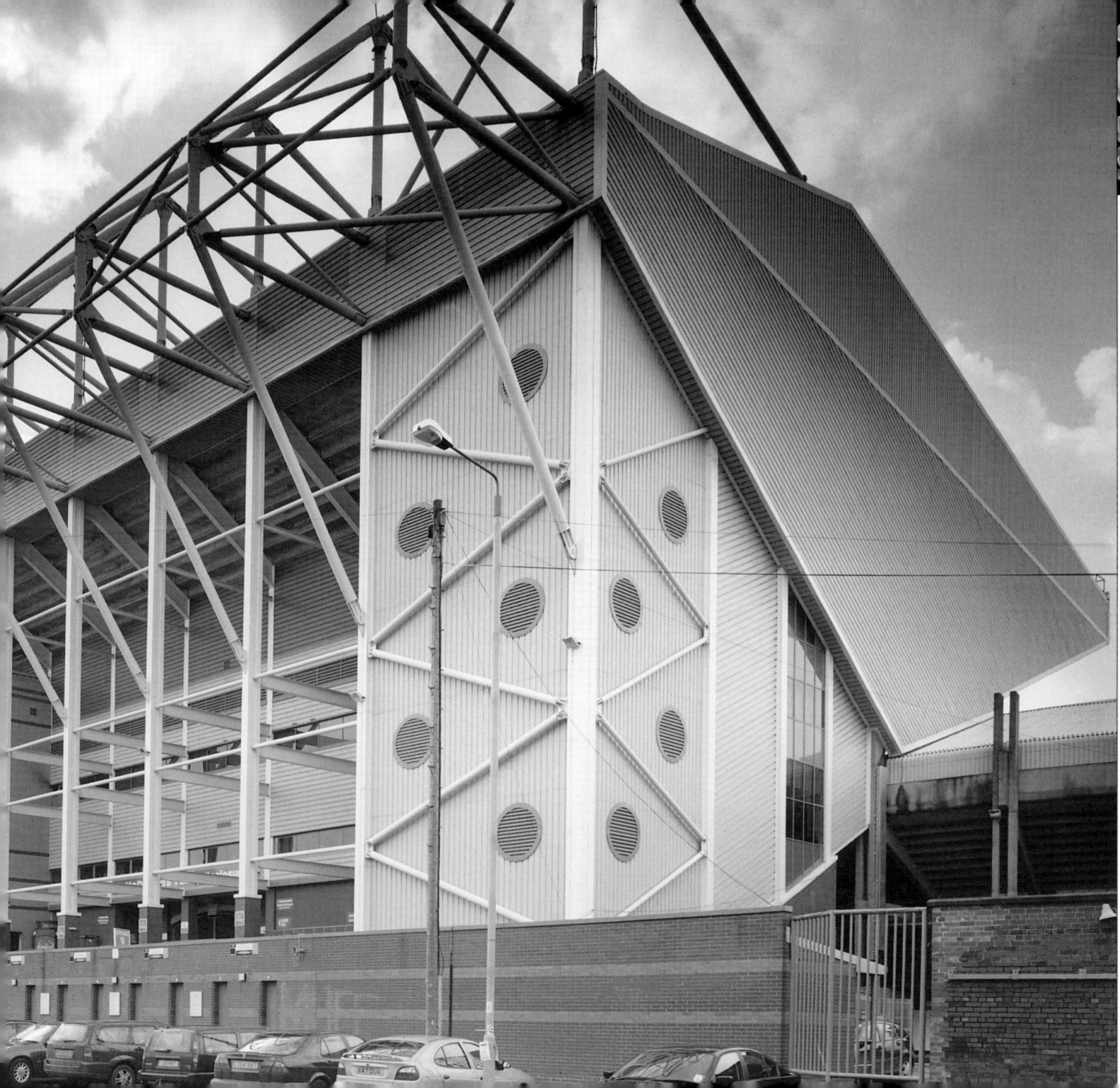

RUTLAND LODGE

Built: 1830's	Location: Junction of Potternewton Lane and Scott Hall Road.

"Grand Victorian house latterly in the care of Leeds City Council. Architectural gem provided extra dimension to ones training sessions at Scott Hall Leisure Centre".

P. Yates

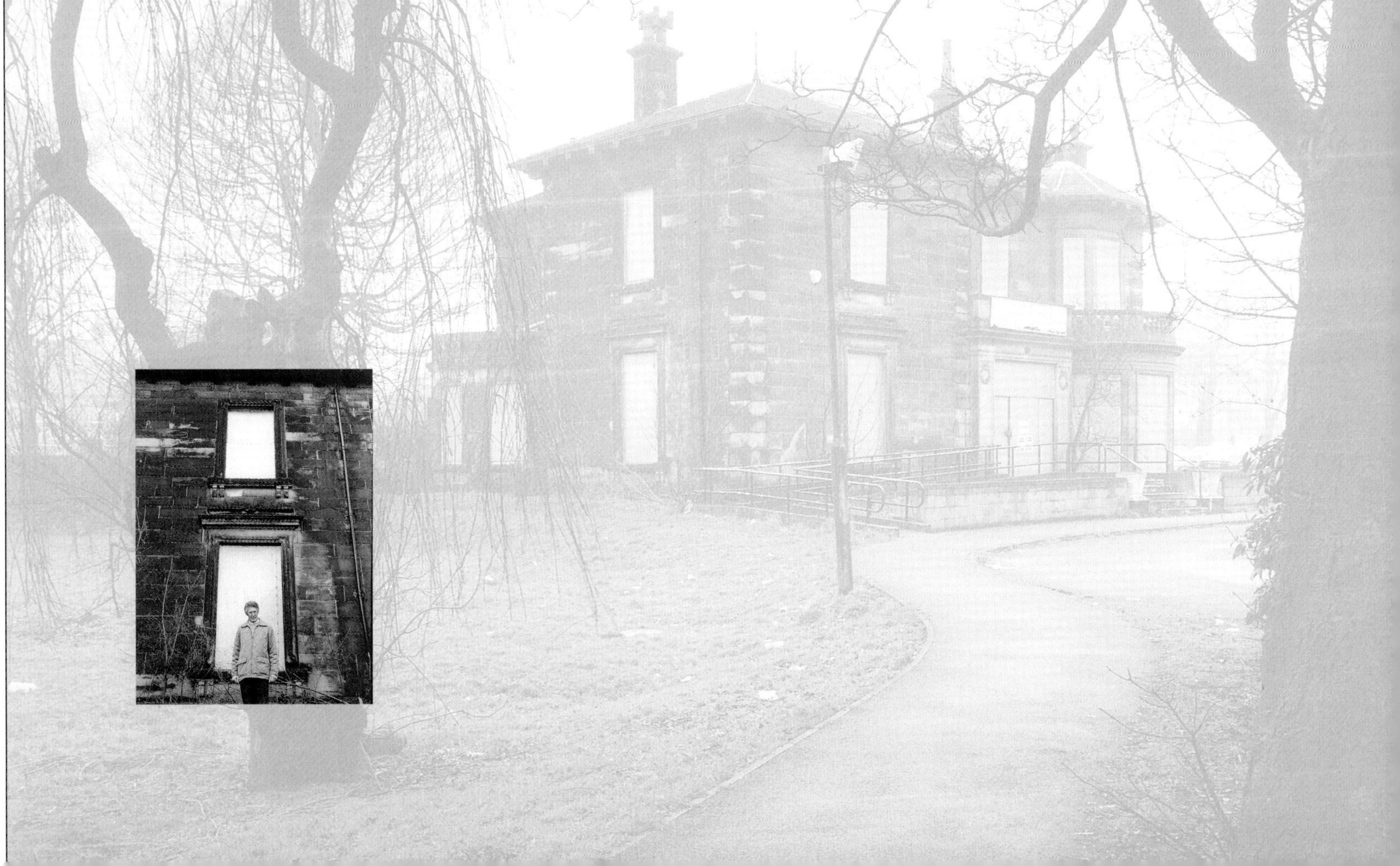

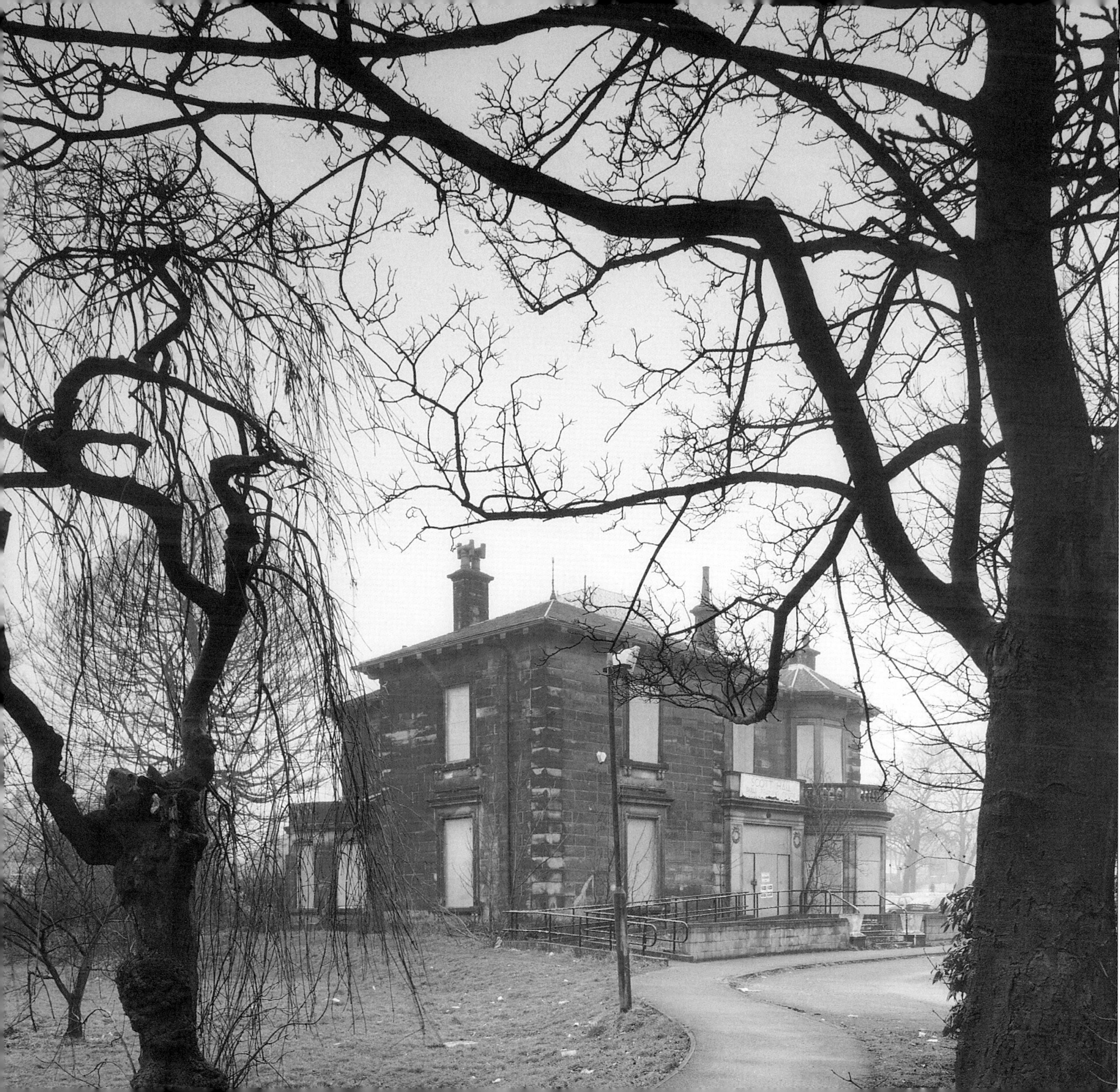
SCOTT HALL

THE WAREHOUSE

Location: Somers Street.

" I love it here, I travel over from Manchester as often as I can. It's much more friendly and people accept you for what you are and I take some accepting, I can tell you".

Waynetta la Freak

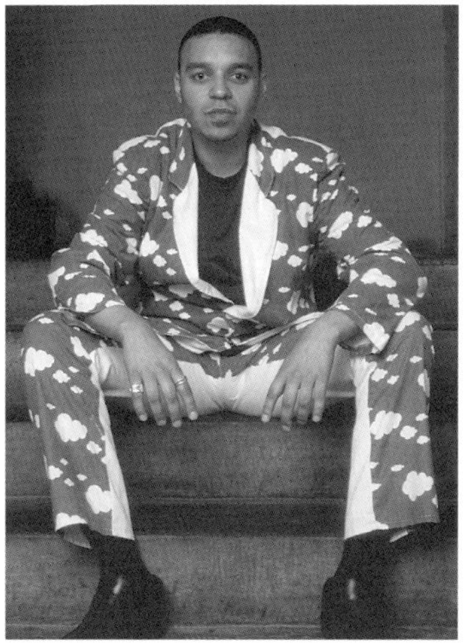

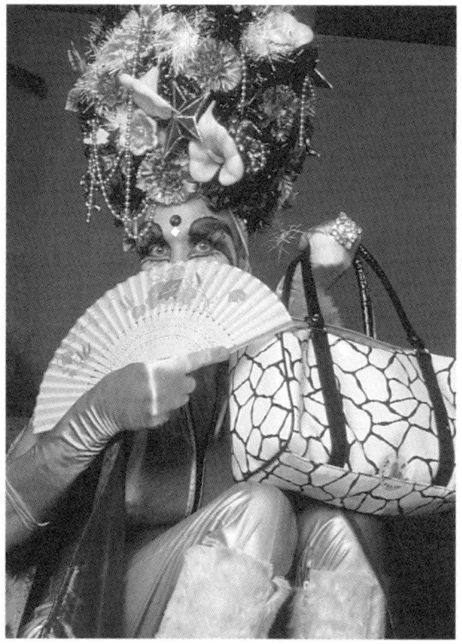

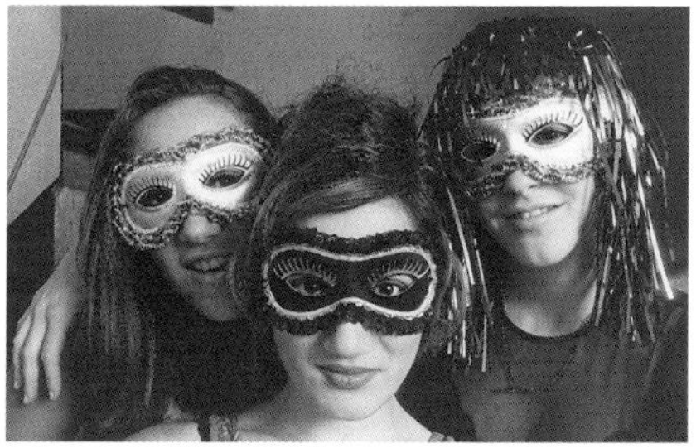

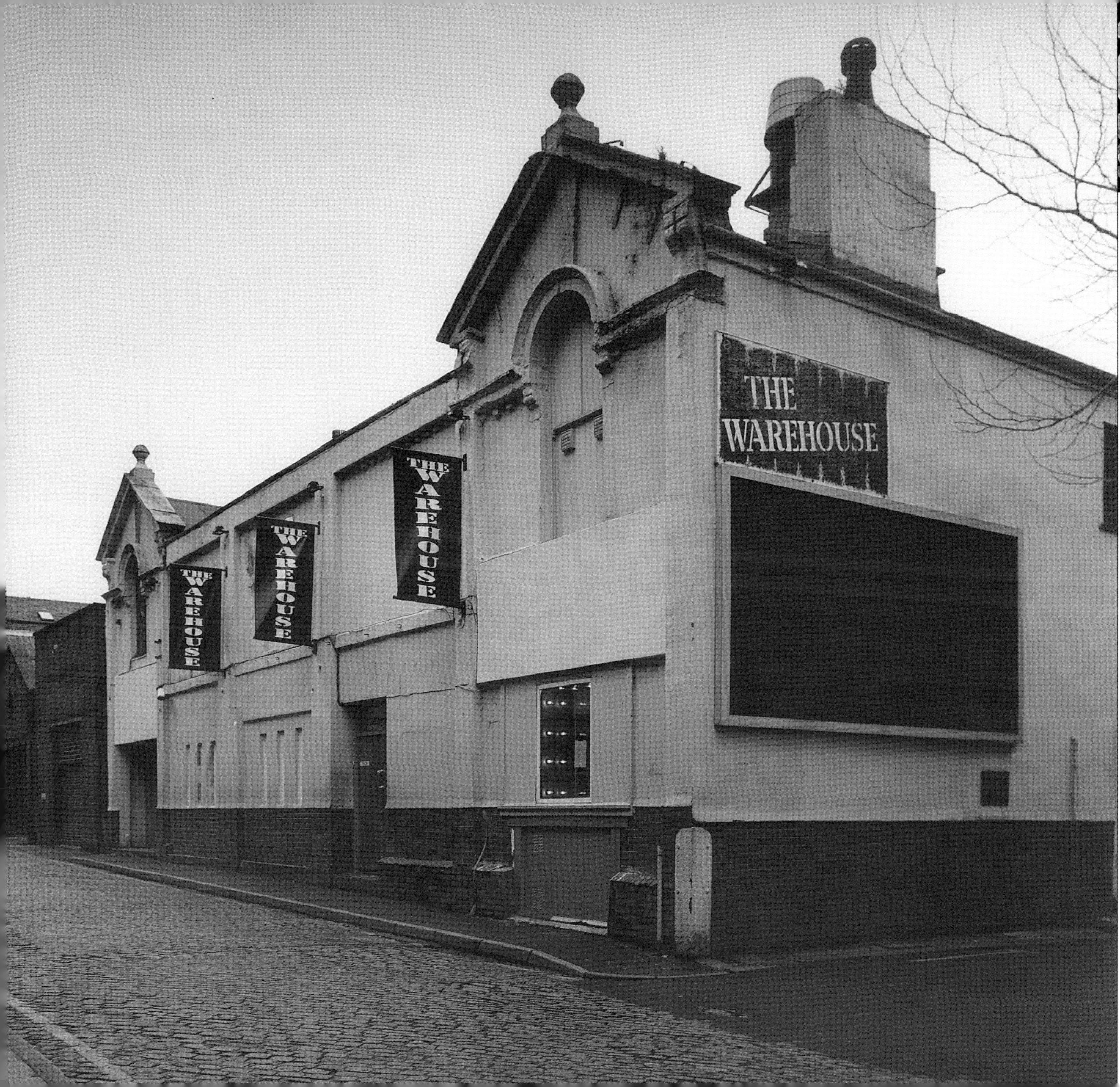
THE WAREHOUSE
THE WAREHOUSE
THE WAREHOUSE
THE WAREHOUSE

THE RAT AND PARROT

Built: 1887.	Location: 43a Woodhouse Lane.	The original Leeds School of Architecture.

"I have many happy memories of this old building, I was a student there and later senior lecturer. 43a was a bit quirky with a lot of character and interest, a few odd corners and a magnificent balconised space which had been the Sunday school hall.

The 1st Year students were in here so we (as staff) could keep our eyes on them! Every Christmas the 1st year students would entertain local children with a party in the hall.

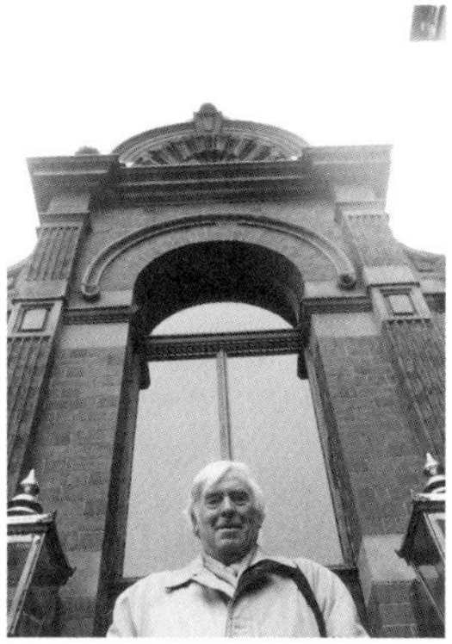

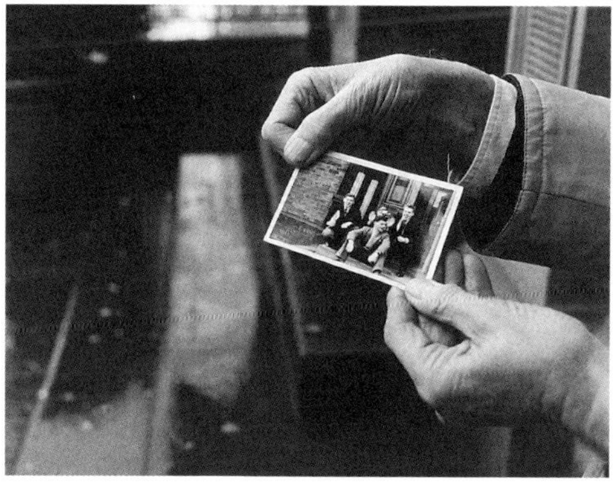

It's wonderful how such a building has survived since 1887 with so many people doing so many different things. It has certainly paid for itself! It has hosted Religion, Art, Architecture, Music and now "The Rat and Parrot", a huge boozing emporium. What would those early worshippers (who had presumably signed the "Pledge") have thought about that?

Brian Godward

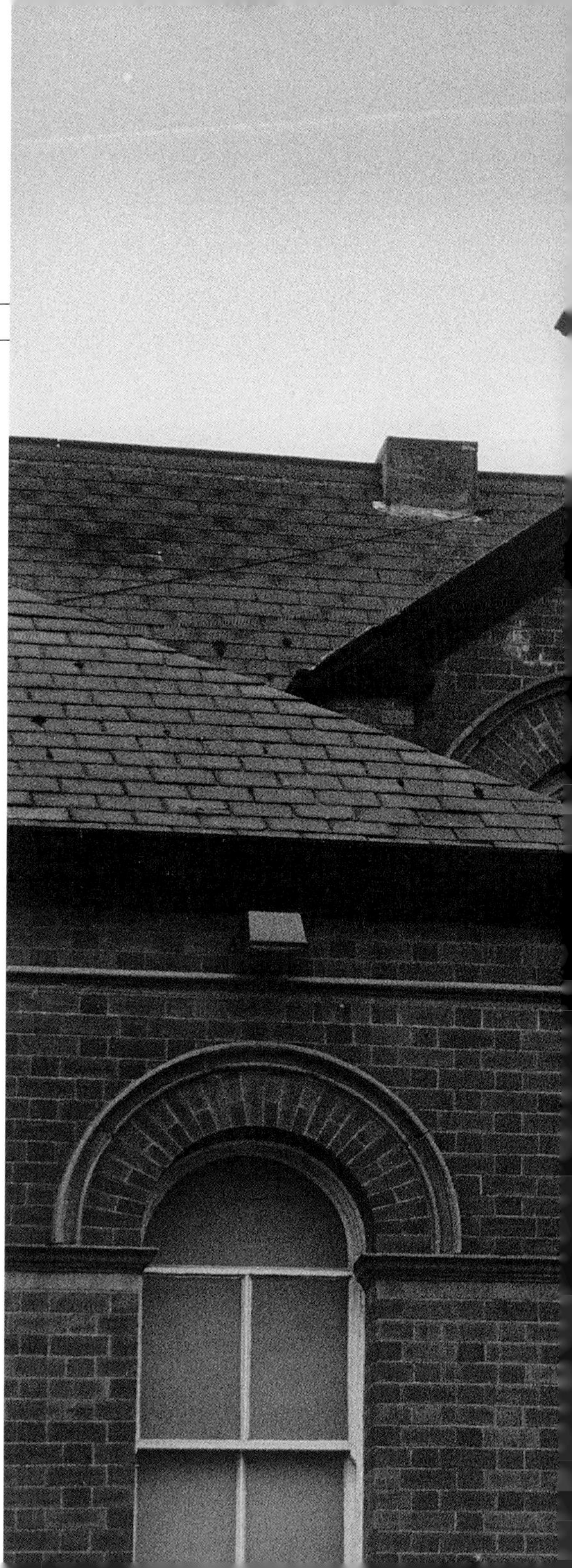

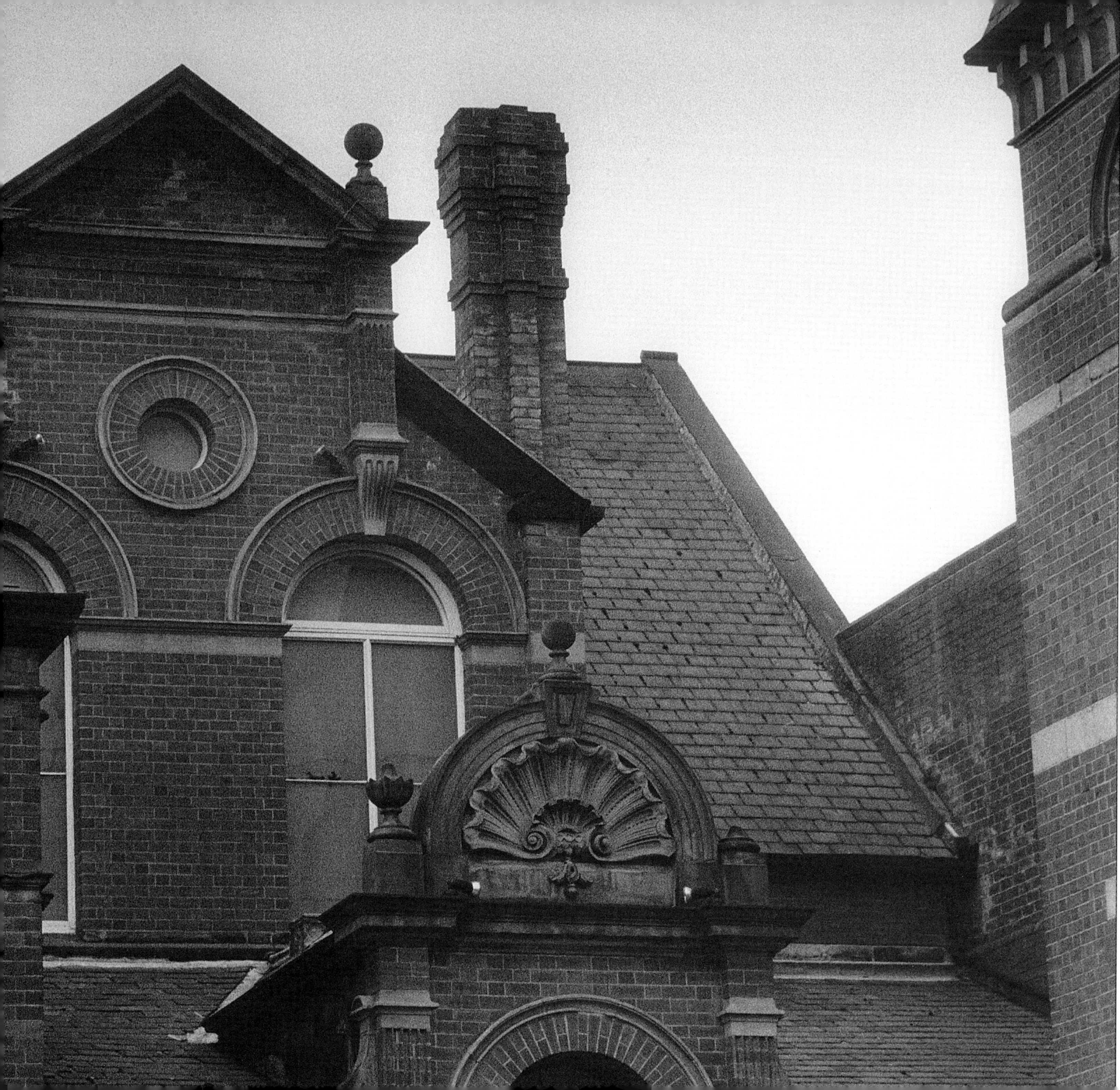

HYDE PARK PICTURE HOUSE

Built: 1908.	Location: Brudenell Road, Hyde Park.

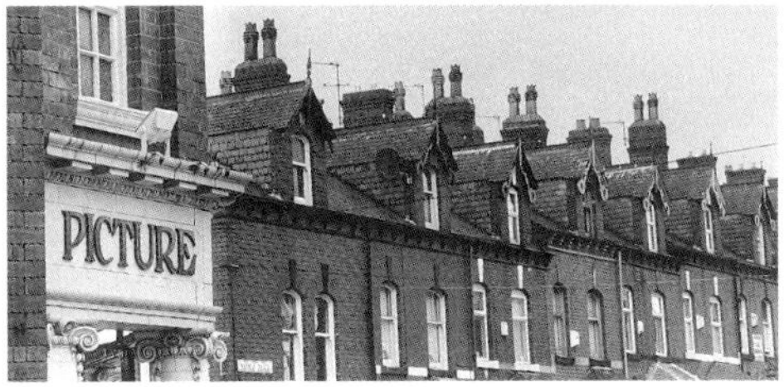

"As a teenager from 1949-1956 I was a frequent attender to see my screen idols, Gregory Peck, Robert Mitchum, Richard Todd, Rita Hayworth, Doris Day and Frank Sinatra.

I used to arrive for 6 pm if possible. If the film had started, an usherette would light the way to a seat with a torch and walk up the aisle selling ice cream. As the performances were continuous and showed an 'A' and 'B' film, I often stayed for the main film to come round again to see more".

Janet Jones

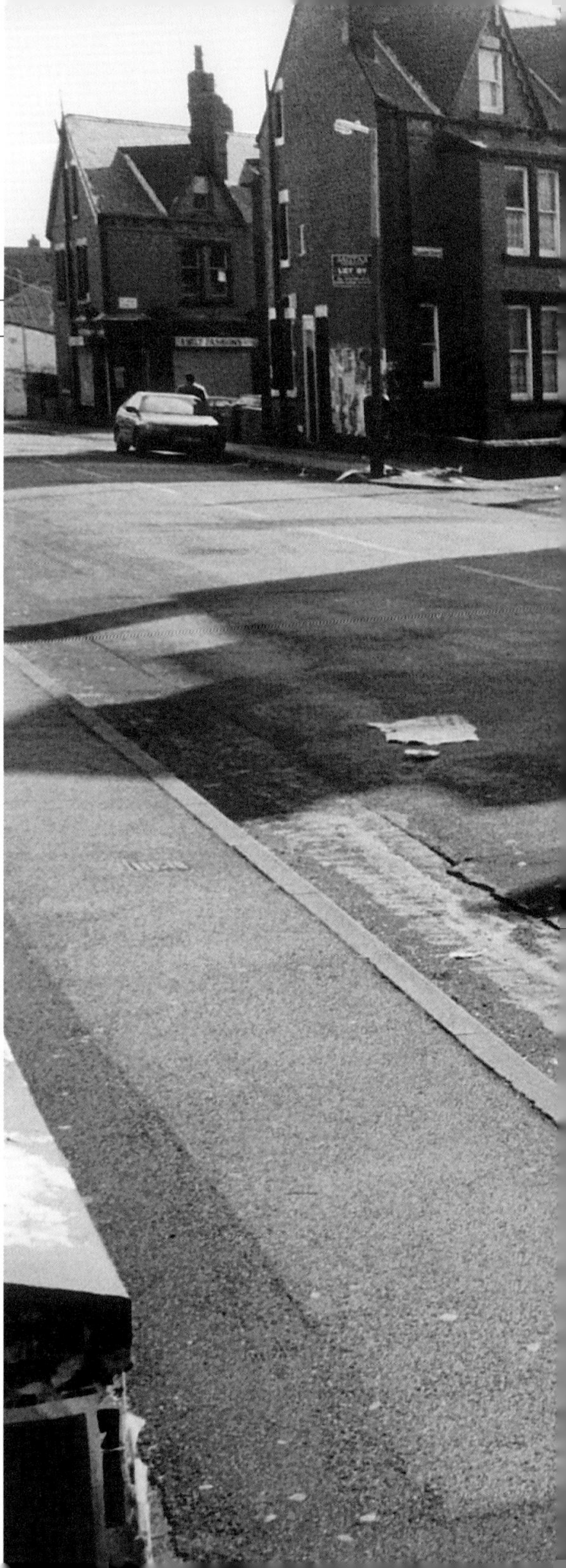

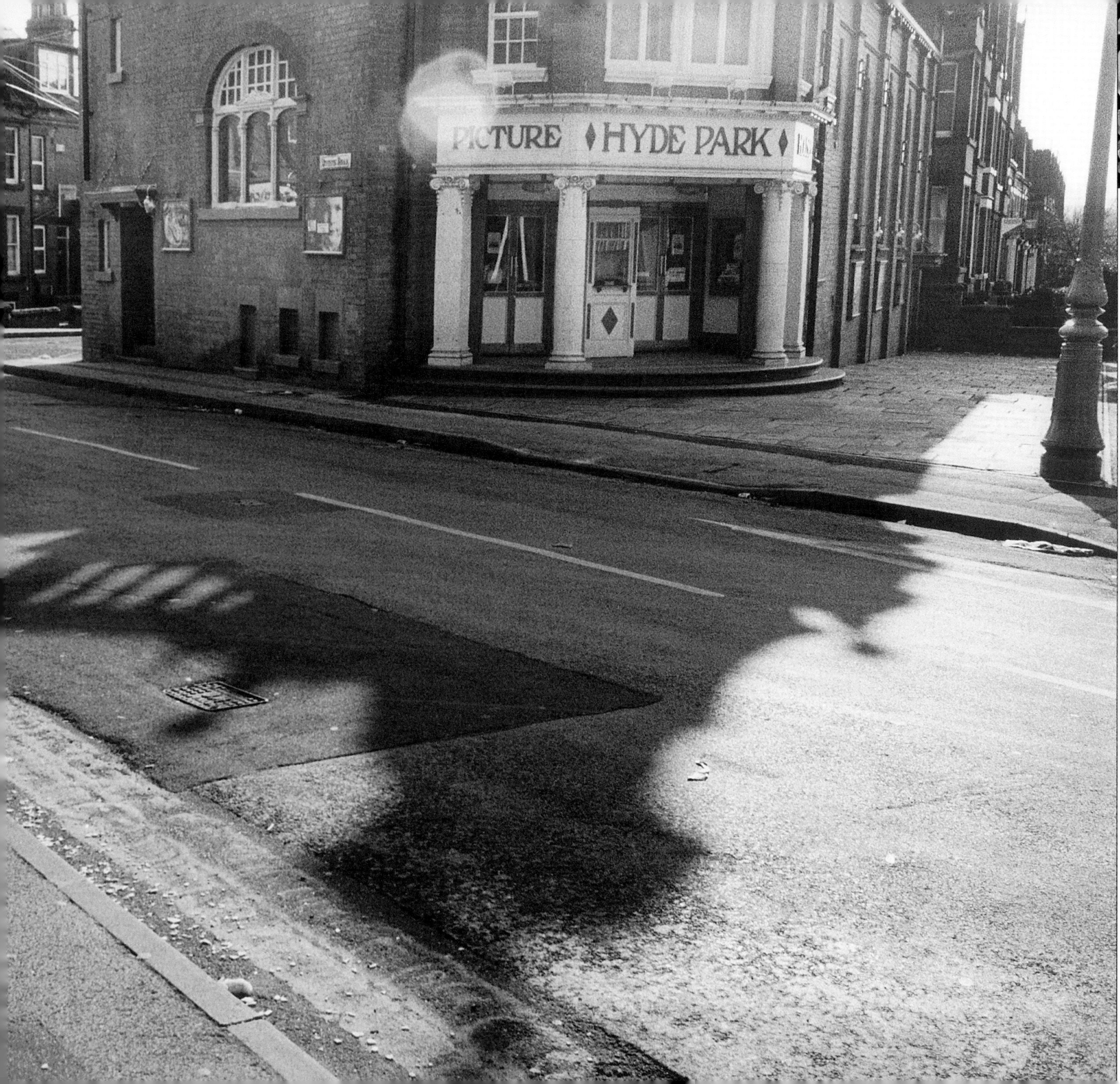
PICTURE
HYDE PARK

CIVIC HALL

Built: 1933 E. Vincent Harris.	Location: Calverley Street.

"Uh if the Council finds two blades of grass, they'll try and build on it, them lovely gardens that were in front of the Civic hall they have gone haven't they?"

Mildred Dunn

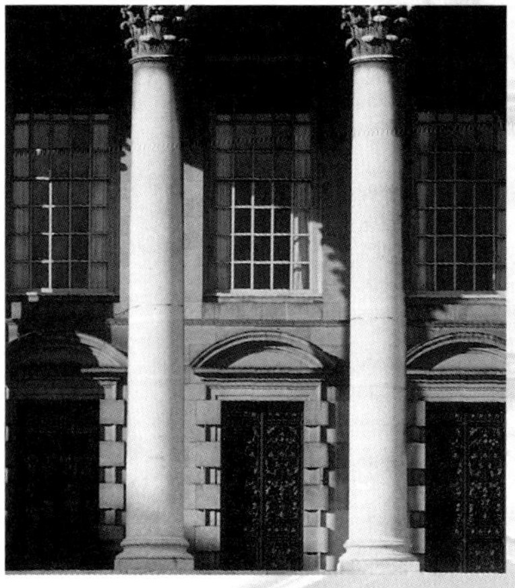

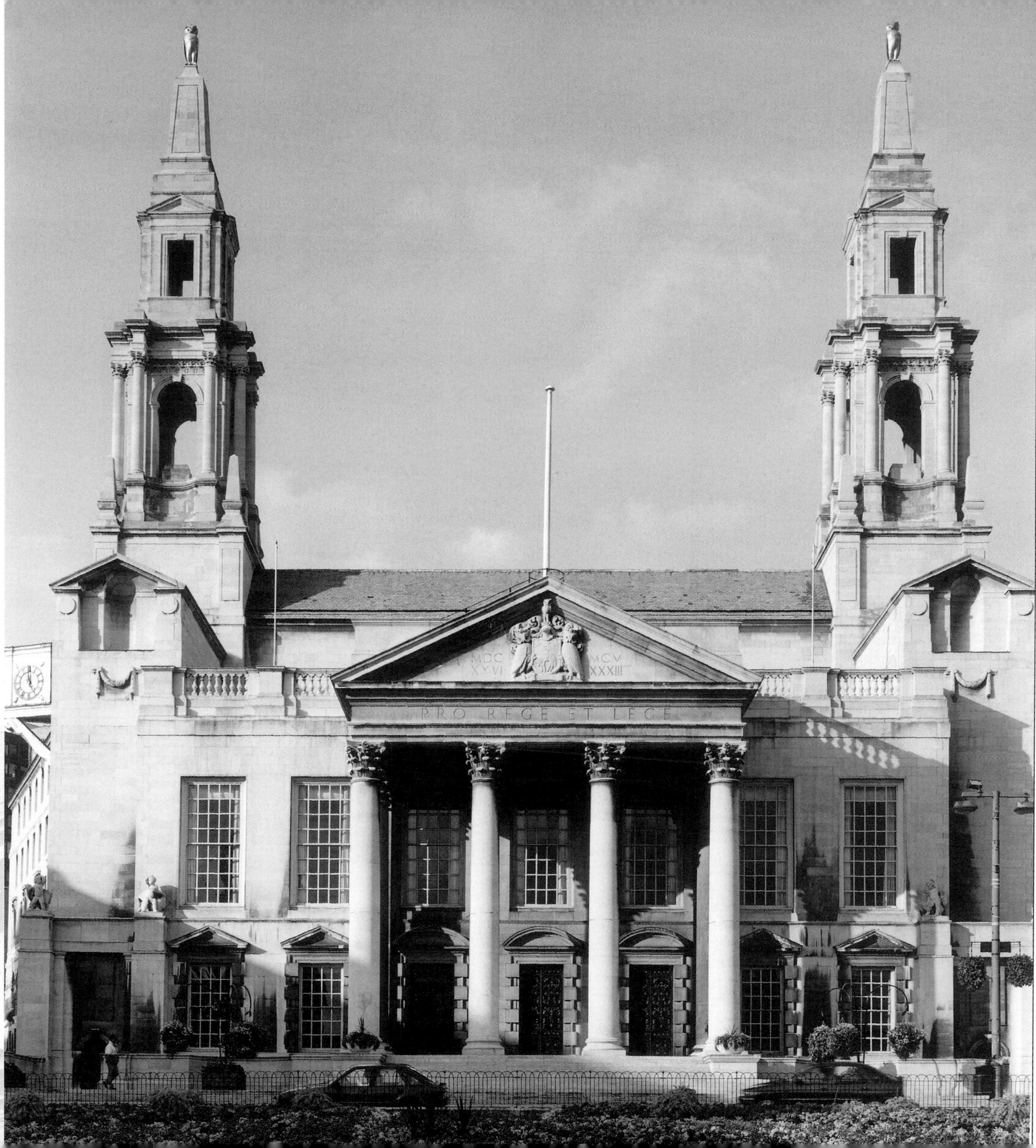
PRO REGE ET LEGE

ARMLEY MILLS

Built: 1805-07 Benjamin Gott.	Location: Canal Road Armley.

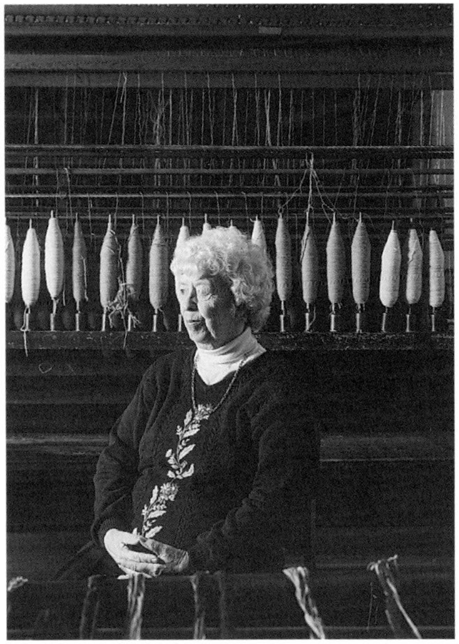

" I worked in the mill at Armley in 1951. I met my husband there and my sister also met her husband there. My mother also worked at the mill, so I have very strong connections with the building.

My husband was the very last worker to leave the mill, helping Geoffrey Tempest (the last owners of the mill were Bentley and Tempest) to clear up when the mill closed down.

I also kept in touch with a gentleman called Ron Toroy who was Bentley and Tempest's chauffeur, and he lived in the house at the mill".

Barbara Gorbun

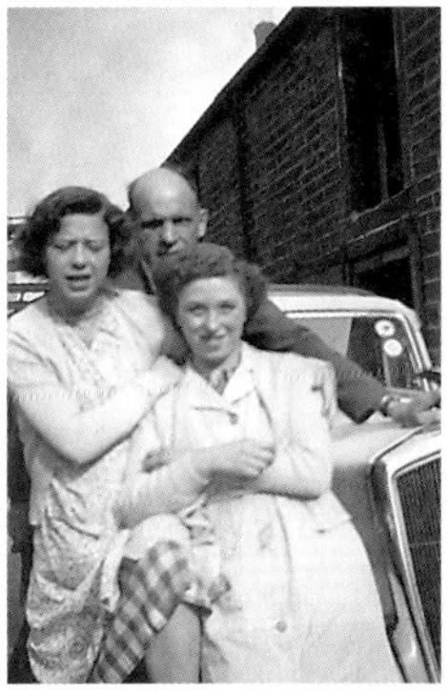

Barbara Gorbun (left) in the mill yard 1951.

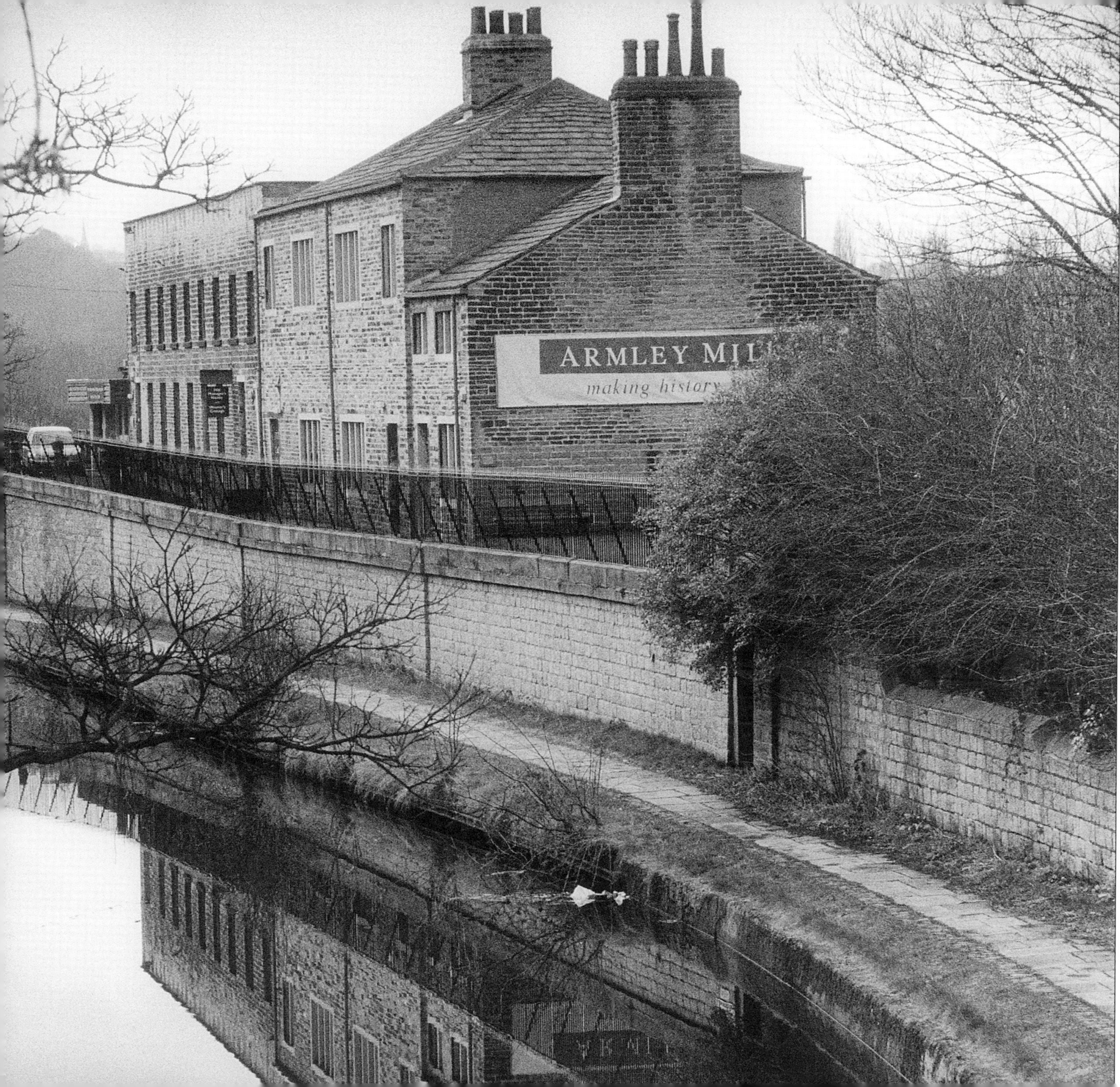
ARMLEY MILL
making history

SLOAN AND DAVIDSON CAST IRON FOUNDRY

Founded: Late 18th century	Location Stanningley.

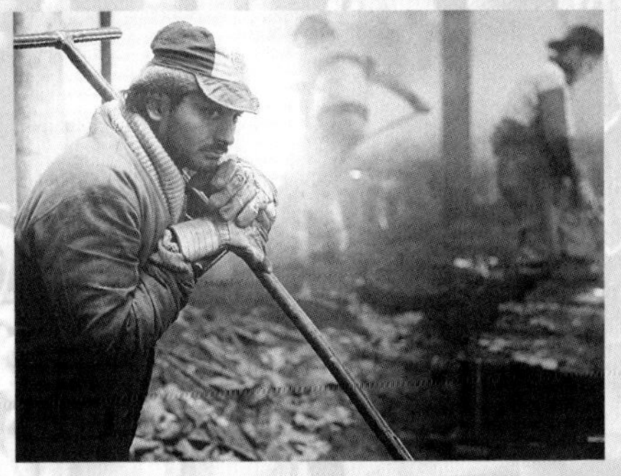

" Its hard work, its hot, its dirty and at the end of a day you are knackered, but I like it. specially if I am out somewhere and I see something that I have made, it gives me a feeling of pride".

A.Khan

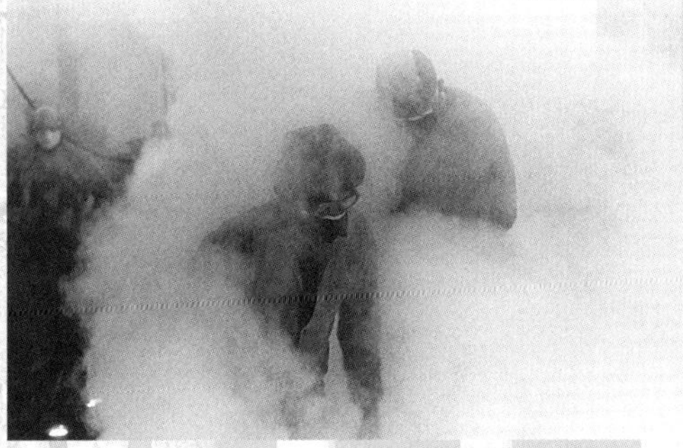

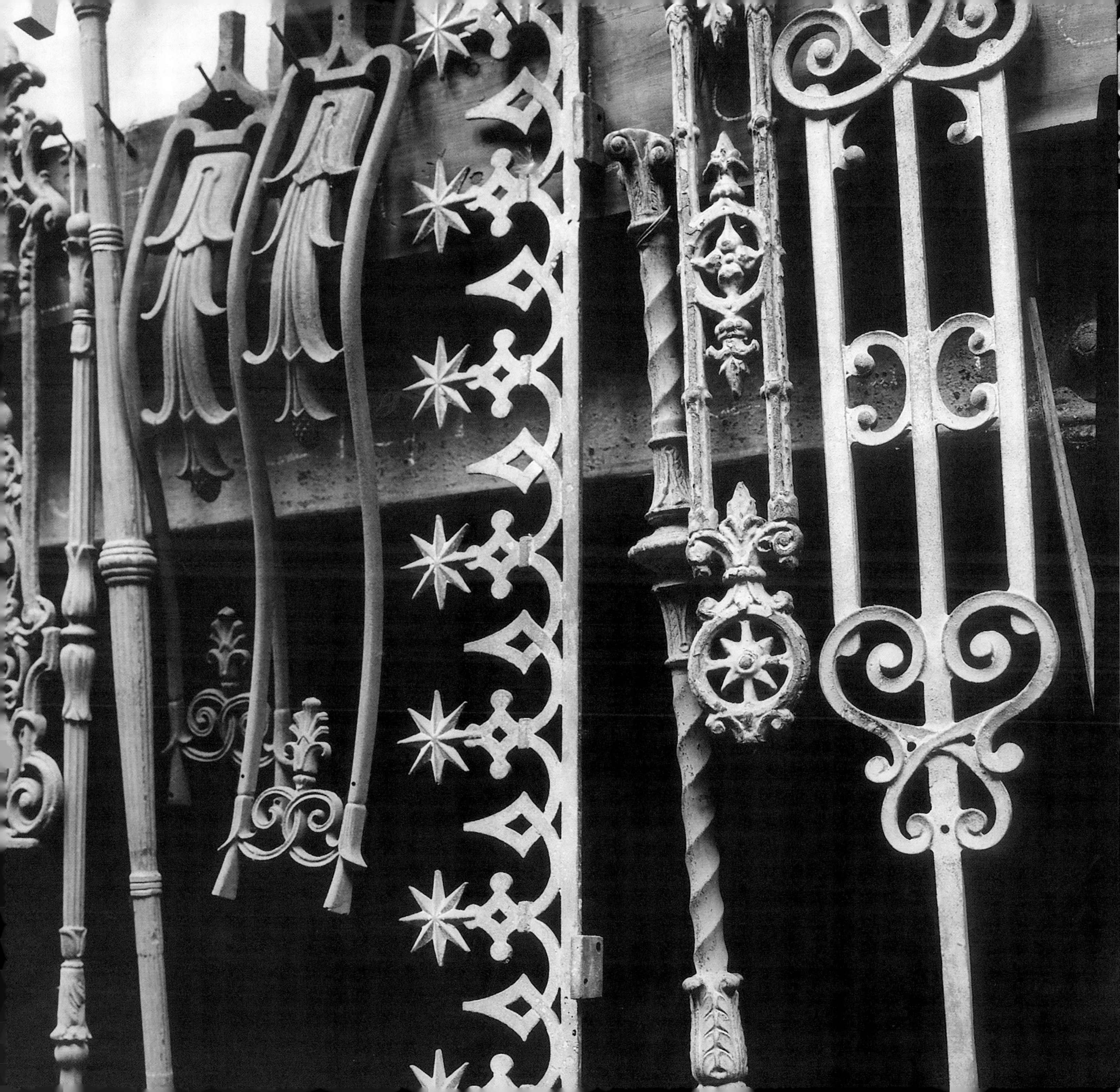

ARMLEY BATHS

Built: 1932.	Location: Carr Crofts Armley.

"I've lived in this house for 30 years since Jimmy Watkinson the previous baths manager retired. The baths opened on the 24th September 1932 with a swimming gala and closed two days later so they could put in the dance floor. The swimming baths used to close September to March, it was too expensive to keep the water warm.

The first time the pool was drained they did it too quickly and all of Town Street was flooded. It used to take a team of 5 workmen 8 to 10 days to put the dance floor in. It was a proper maple sprung dance floor. It was built on a trestle like construction with wooden uprights and steel RSJ's.

I used to be a member of what was called the "crazy gang" we used to provide the entertainment at the swimming galas, well swimming galas can be a bit boring , so we would liven them up a bit by doing all sorts of crazy things. I would ride a bike off the top board, dive into fires of naphthalene floating on the surface, perform comic water ballets etc. Once I appeared as Ivan Awfulitch, the Russian Champion. We rigged a rope underwater that went along the racing lane and into one of the access tunnels at the side of the baths. In the tunnel was a team of men ready to pull the rope when the race began. I made my entrance on the shoulders of another man, we had an enormous overcoat on so we looked like a giant, we tripped and fell in the pool, the other man hid under the floating overcoat whilst I attached the rope to a special harness we had borrowed from the Fire Brigade. The race started and the other swimmers were half way up the pool when the team pulled the rope and I shot up the pool in 3.45 seconds winning the race".

Billy Gregg (Mr. Bath-house)

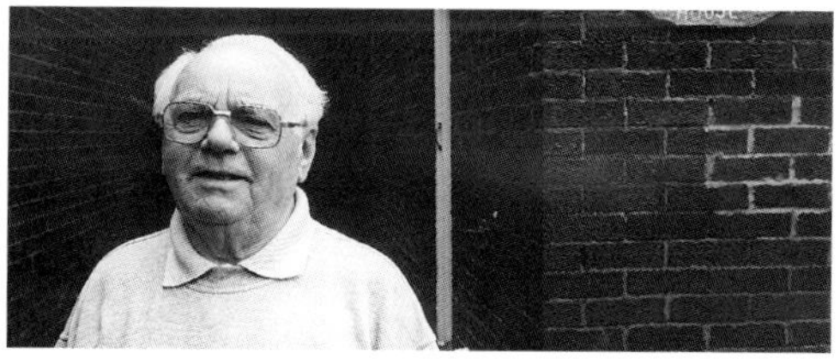

"I can remember learning to swim there, clinging on to my mothers woollen costume and screaming down the length of the pool! I took part in many galas between 1939 and 1950. There were all sorts of competitions, comic diving, races, polo, etc. The one I particularly remember was the "Plunging competition" it was always won by a big lady called Mrs. Wood, the competition was to dive in and see who could swim the furthest underwater.

I was a member of Armley Ladies, but there was Armley Midgets for children and Armley Leander was the men's team. As well as the swimming baths there were Russian baths which were good for getting the Armley and Wortley grime out of your skin".

Marie Phillips

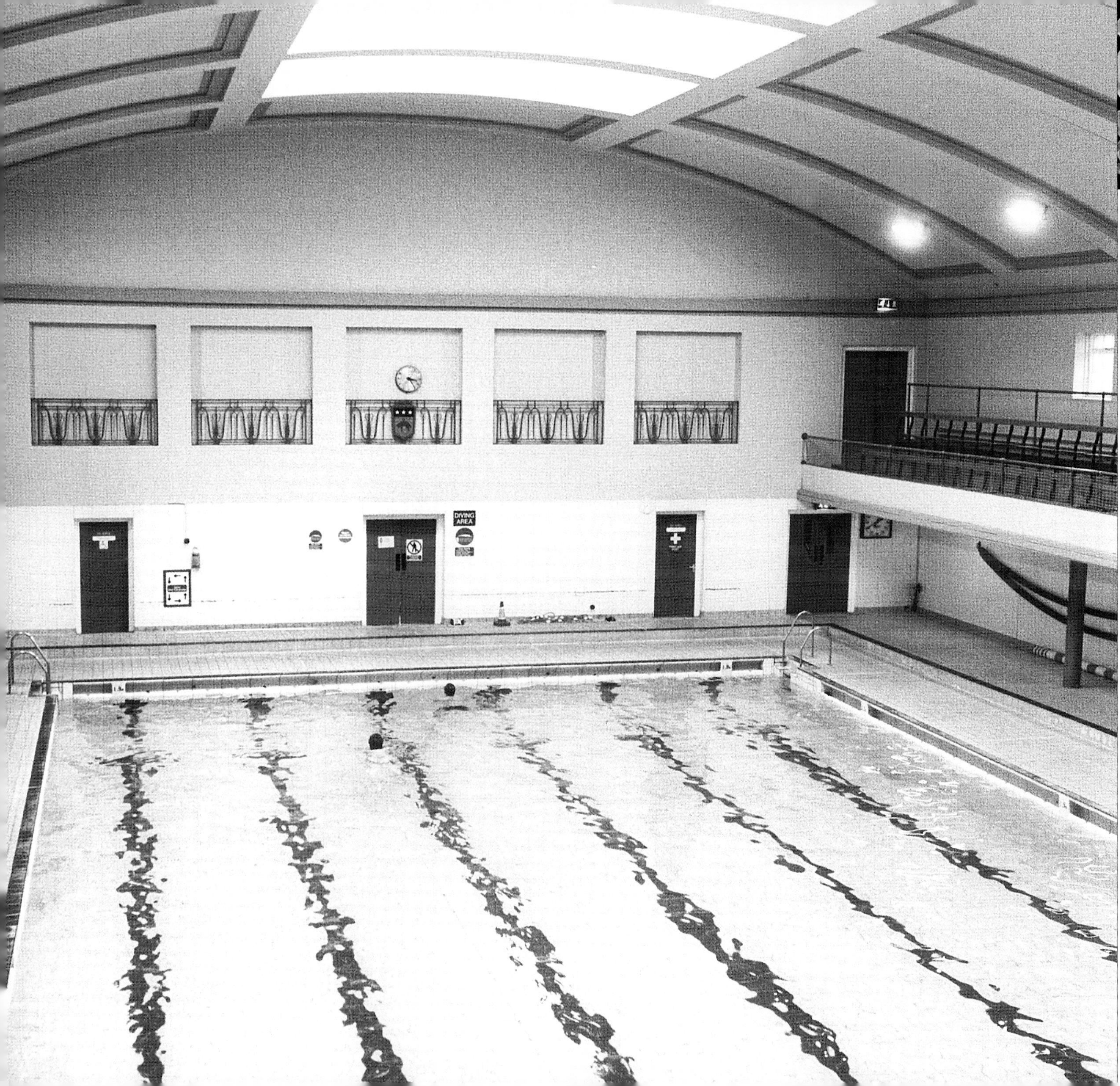
DIVING
AREA

GRIFFIN HOTEL

Built: 1860's	Location : Corner of Mill Hill and Boar Lane.

"The Griffin Hotel Boar Lane, I worked there for a time, I liked it, it was exciting. The Australian Cricket Team stayed there, they had some lovely dinners, one night they wanted oysters, well we had none, so we had to send a lad down to the market to get some.

I worked there for 6 months 17/6 a week I was paid. I left because they wanted me to sleep in, that's fatal, they would have you working all the time".

Mildred Dunn

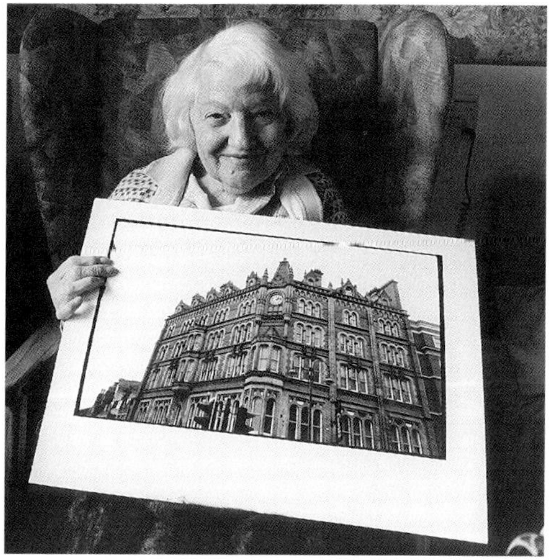

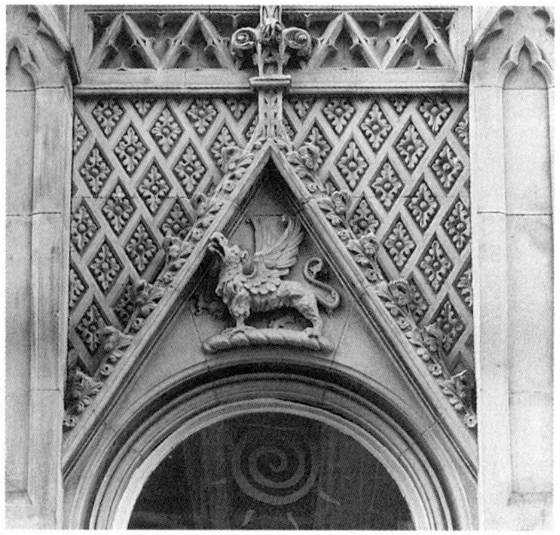

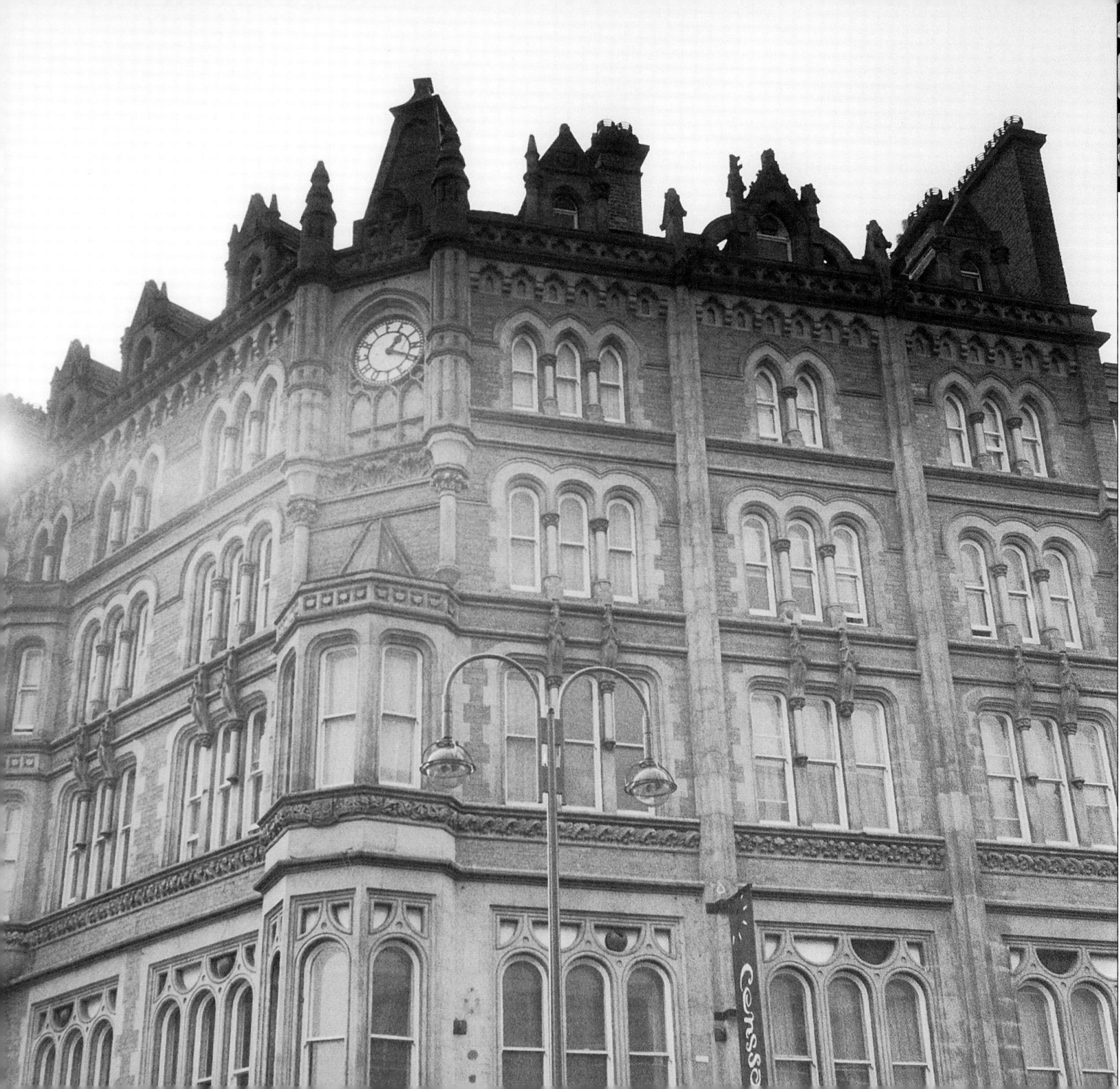

YEADON TARN

Location: Cemetery Road, Yeadon.

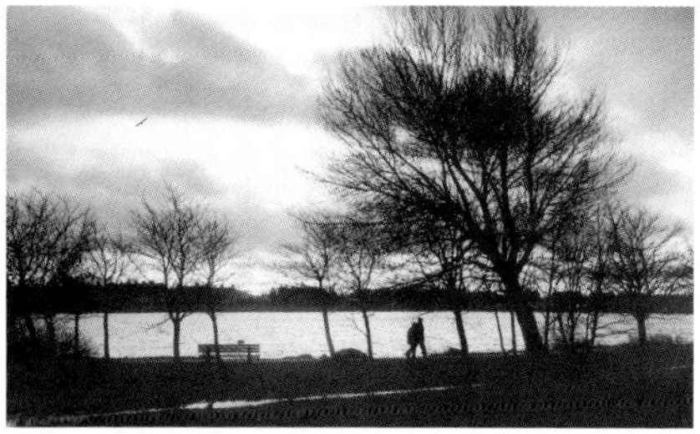

"I was born right opposite Yeadon Tarn in Cemetery Road, imagine how cheerful my childhood was with funerals going past every day. I was a lonely child, I would sit on the wall looking at the tarn and blowing bubbles through an old clay pipe that my Grandfather gave me. It seemed to me that the tarn would freeze every Winter and all the kids would go skating I would have loved to have a go, but I had no skates.

When I was 16 my Dad bought a tandem, he wanted to keep me off the street corners, and he thought that cycling would do me good. All I thought about was getting my arms brown. We would cycle over to Bolton abbey and Burnsall on Sundays, it was beautiful. There were no cars around then. We joined the CTC (Cycle Touring Club), you could stay in a B & B for 3/6.

All this was before the War in the 1920s. I have always had a soft spot for the Tarn, it brings back lots of happy memories".

Bessie Rowlands

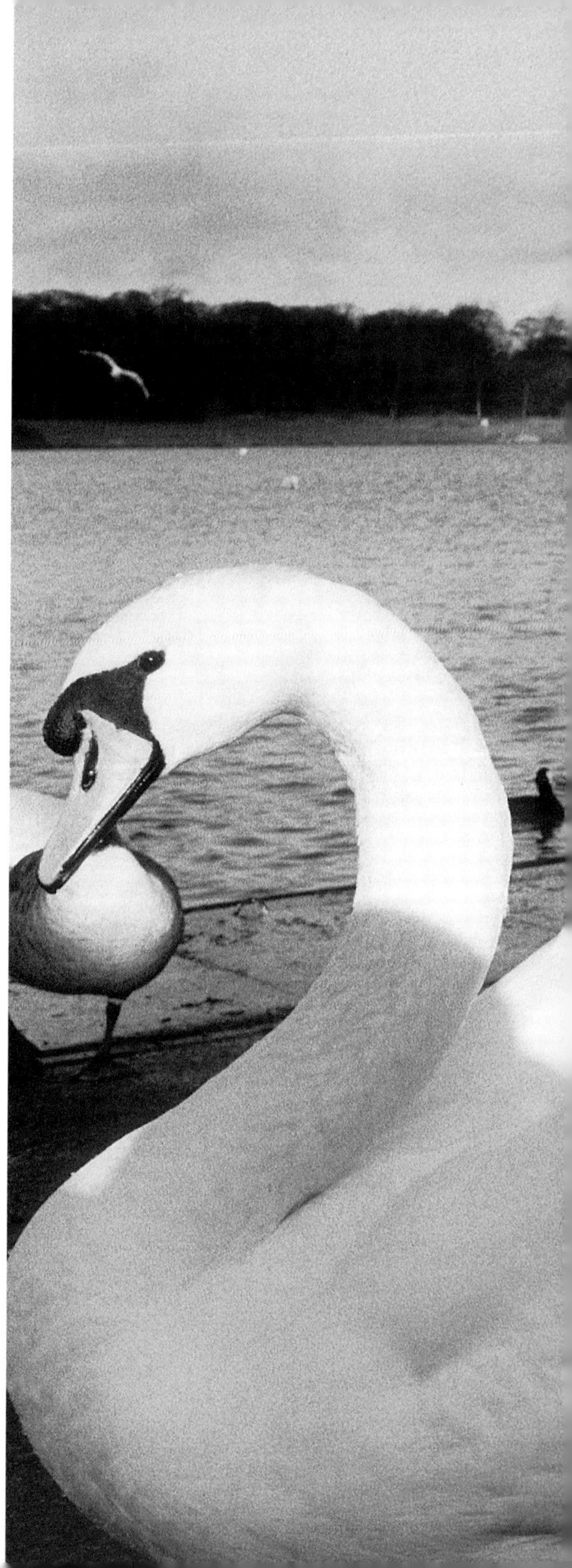

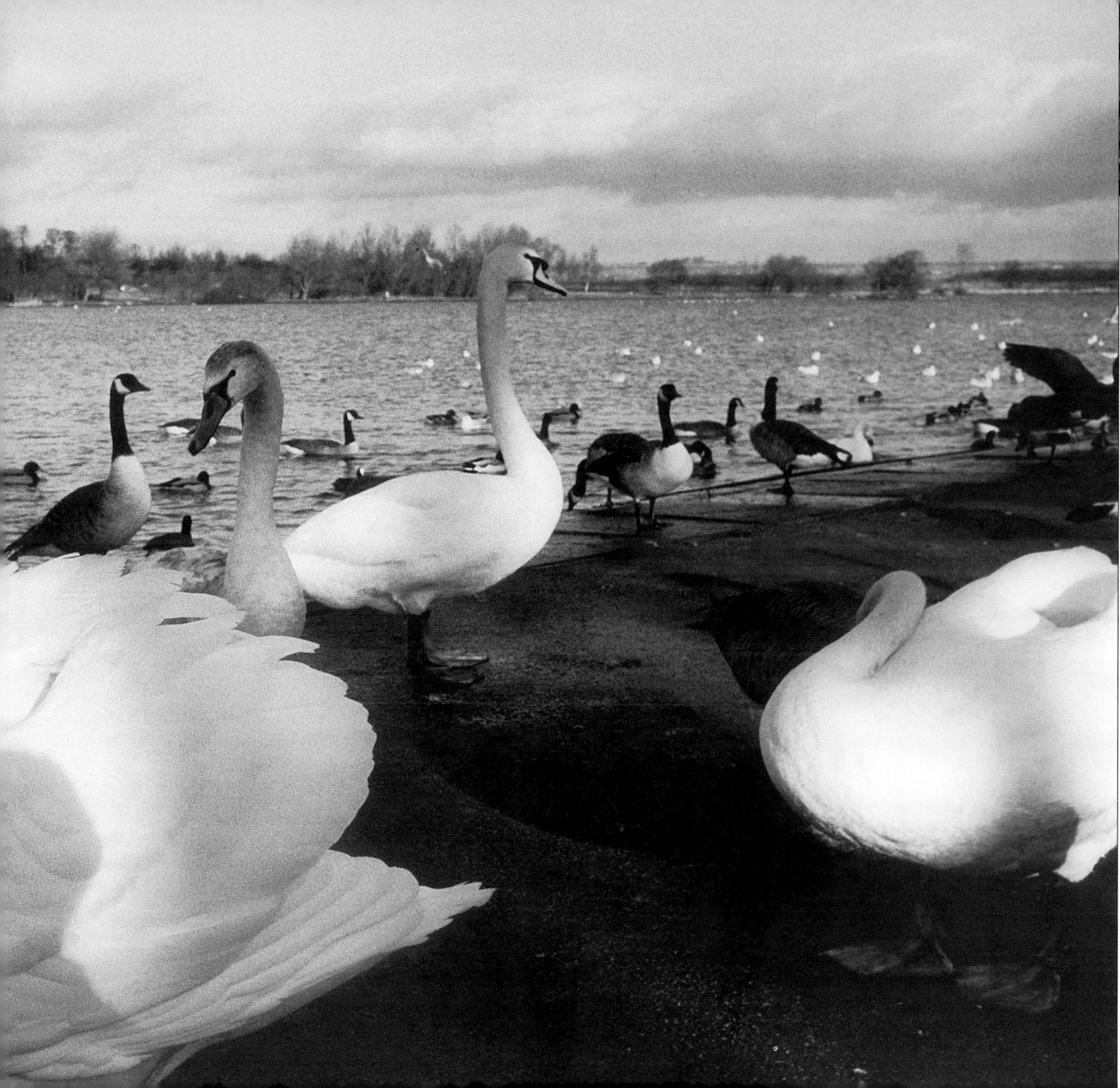

THE LEEDS LIVERPOOL CANAL

Built: 1775 to 1800.	Location: Near Globe Road.

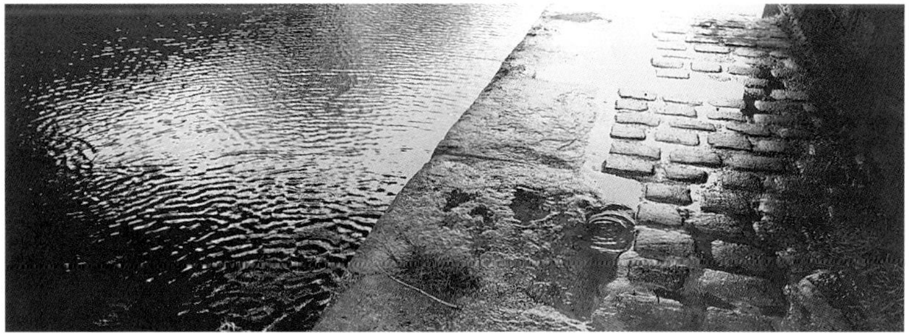

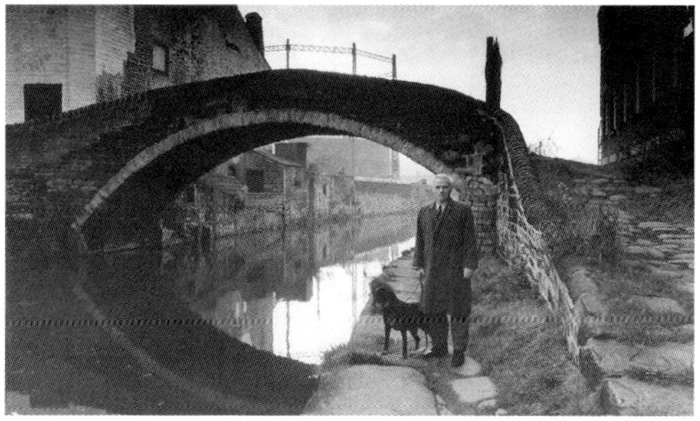

"I walk miles along the towpath. It is good walking, steady not too hard. There is no danger of being run over. There is plenty to see, wildlife and you get a different view of the city".

John Smith

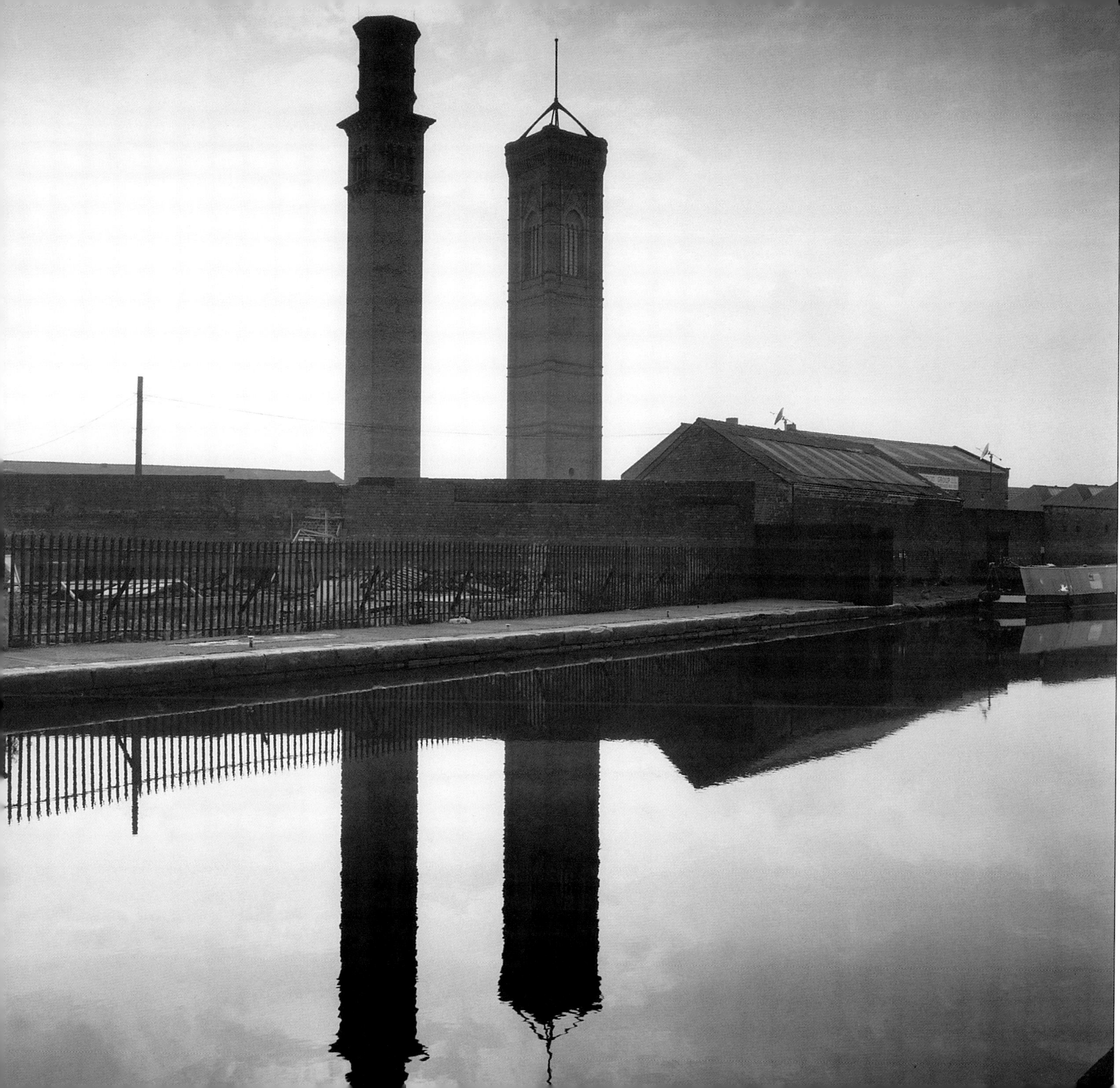

KIRKSTALL ABBEY

Built: 1152.	Location: Kirkstall Road.

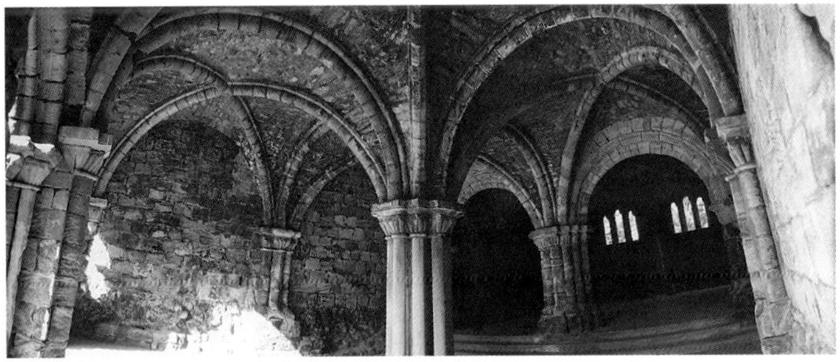

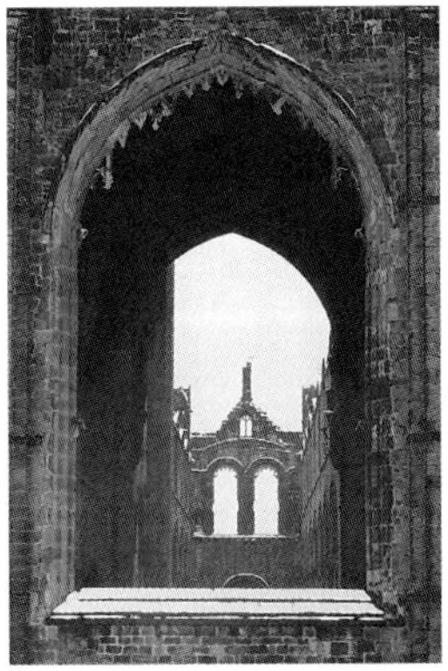

"I love Kirkstall Abbey. I couldn't believe that anything as old and atmospheric as Kirkstall Abbey existed just 15 minutes outside the city centre. We take the dog there most Sunday afternoons.

I've heard of couples who use it on an evening too - maybe that's what they mean when they call Leeds a 24 hour city!"

Alison Watson

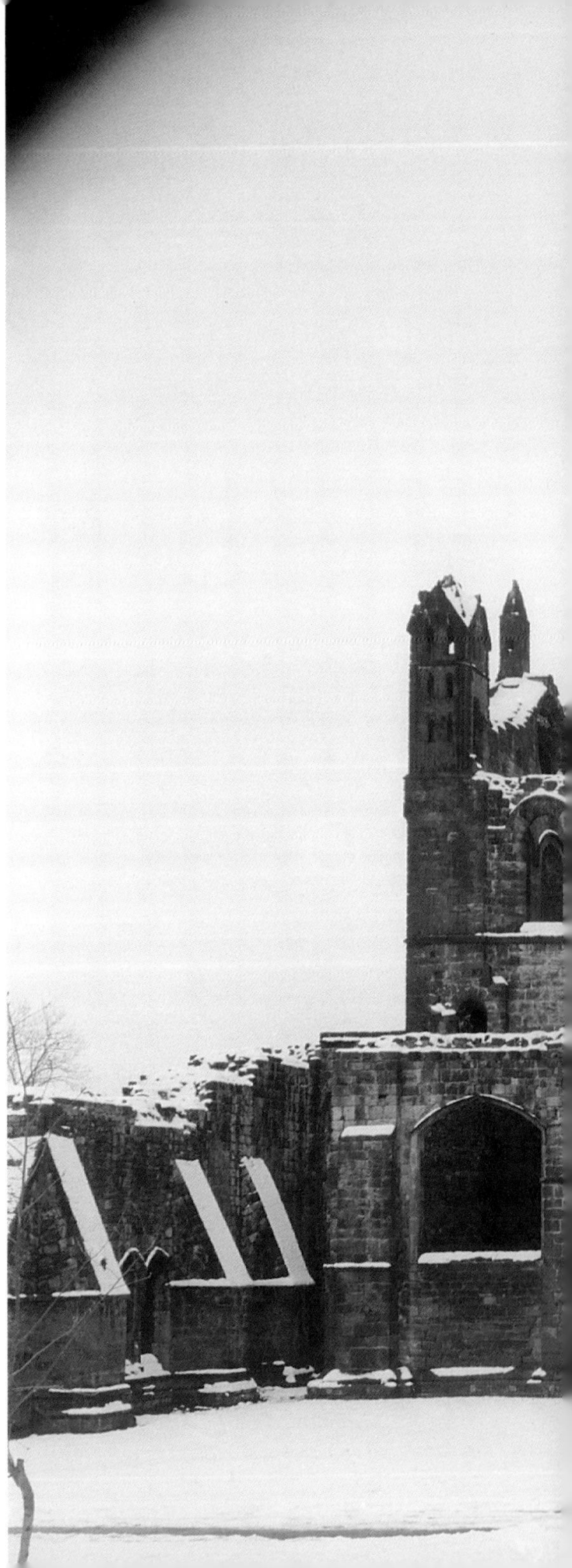

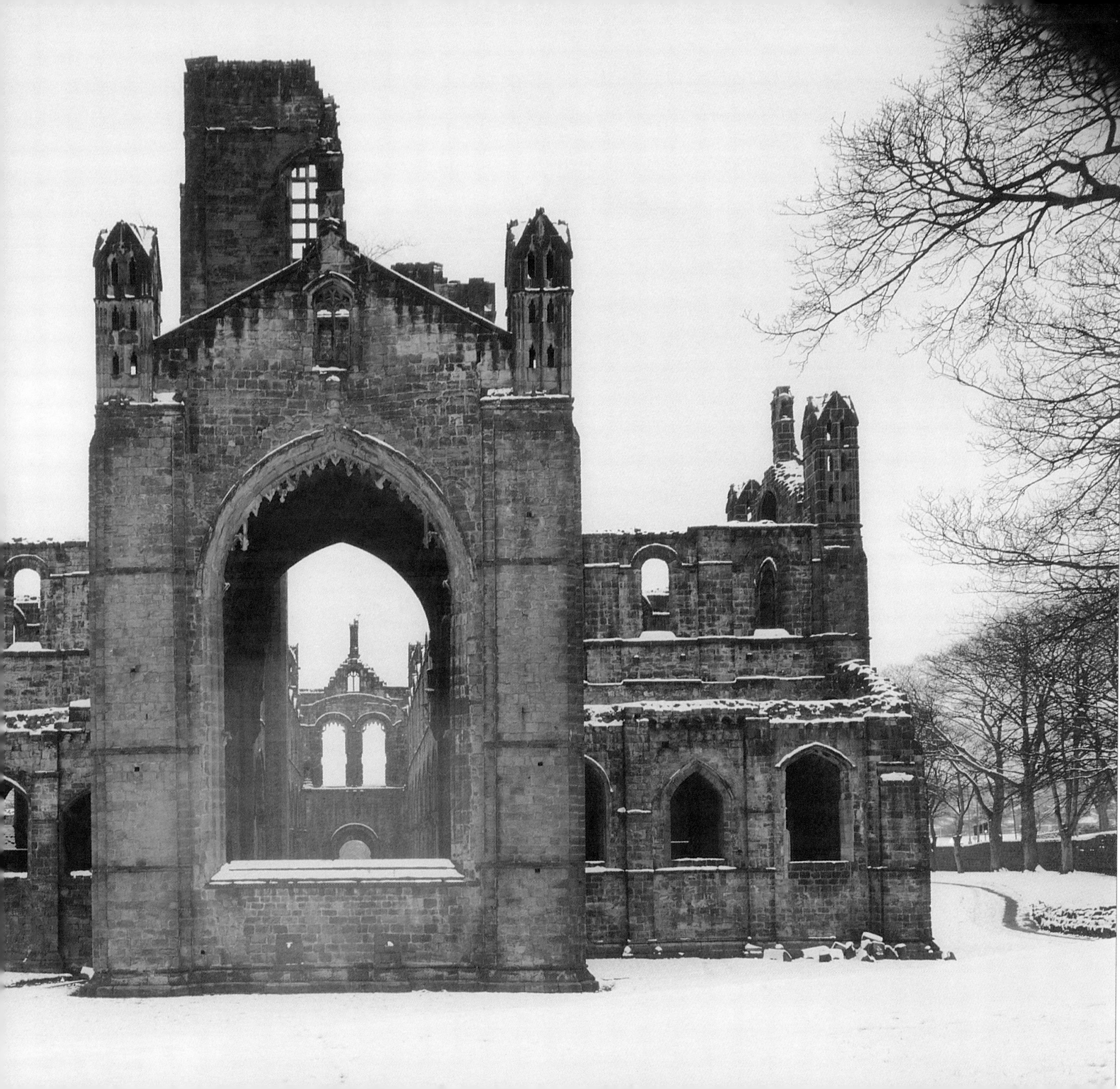

MARKS AND SPENCERS

Built: 1960's.	Location: Albion Street.

"It's the best building in Leeds, the staff are really friendly and supportive. One of my regulars takes me there for a meal now and then. It's not like some of the other places in Leeds they won't let you in because you're a Big Issue seller.

It's not the building that is important, it's the people inside that count".

Matthew Holroyd

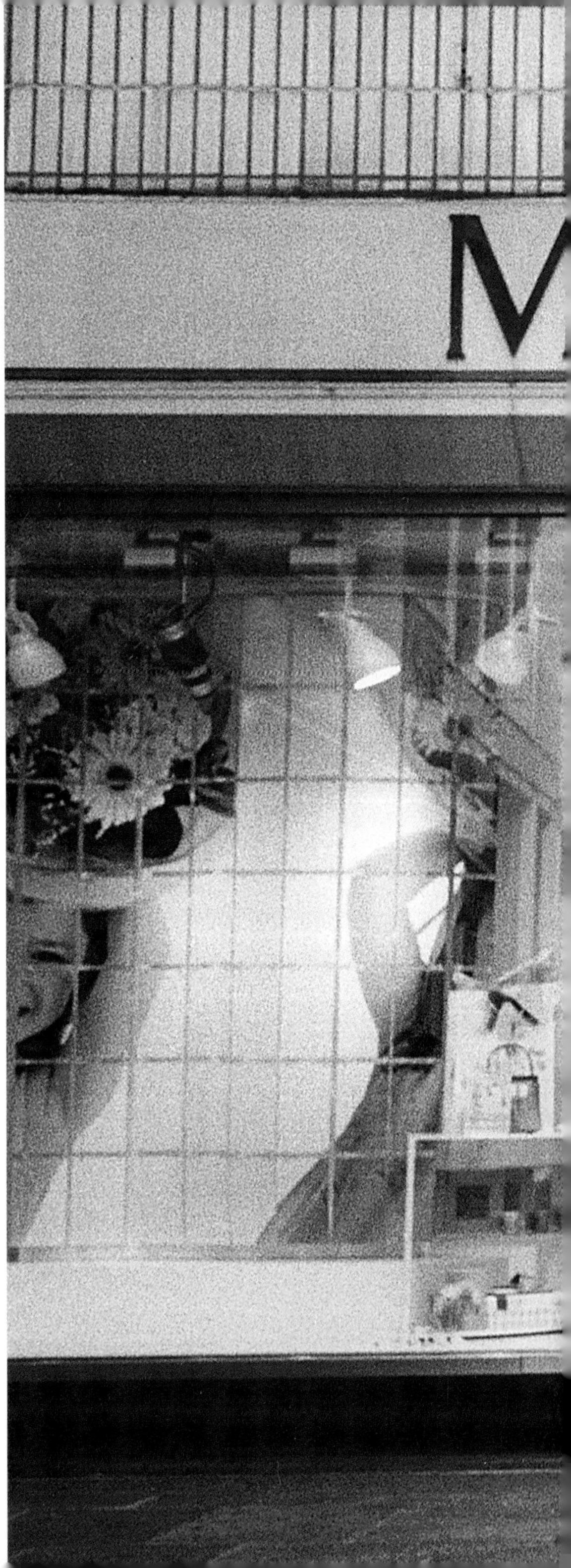